PEARL HARBOR
IN THE
MOVIES

PEARL HARBOR
IN THE
MOVIES

ED RAMPELL
AND LUIS I. REYES

MUTUAL
PUBLISHING

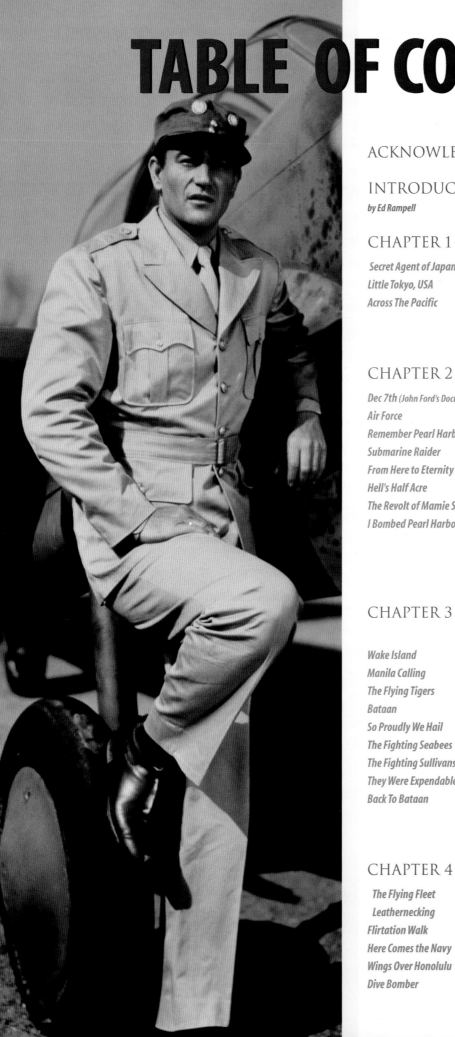

TABLE OF CONTENTS

CHAPTER 5 **Pearl Harbor on Television**   97

CHAPTER 6 **Documentaries**   111

CHAPTER 7 **Roll Call of Pearl Harbor Screen Heroes**   125
by Luis I. Reyes

BIBLIOGRAPHY   130

VIDEOGRAPHY   132
by Luis I. Reyes

AUTHOR BIOS   136

REMEMBER PEARL HARBOR

DONALD M. BARRY
ALAN CURTIS
FAY McKENZIE
IAN KEITH

A R

PEARL

The infamous Japanese attack on Pearl Harbor transforms the romantic island of Hawaii into a living inferno, shatters the lives and loves of three couples, and ends forever America's age of innocence. Starring Angie Dickinson, Dennis Weaver, Robert Wagner and Lesley Ann Warren.
Airing on the ABC Television Network, Thursday, November 16 / Friday, November 17 / Sunday, November 19, 1978.

COLUMBIA PICTURES presents

FROM HERE TO ETERNITY

Starring

BURT LANCASTER · MONTGOMERY CLIFT

DEBORAH KERR · FRANK SINATRA · DONNA REED

Screen Play by DANIEL TARADASH · Based upon the novel by JAMES JONES

Produced by BUDDY ADLER · Directed by FRED ZINNEMANN

PRINTED IN U.S.A.

MAHALO NUI LOA

ACKNOWLEDGMENTS

THIS BOOK WAS the idea of veteran Rob Vampotic, Ed Rampell's brother-in-law, who suggested the concept at a New Year's Eve party, Dec. 31, 2000. No Rob, no book.

SPECIAL THANKS TO

Mike Hawks, Peter Bateman, Larry Edmund's Book Store, Eddie Brandt's Saturday Matinee, Collectors Book Store, Leith Adams of the Warner Bros. Corporate Archive and Museum, Carol Marsh; the Historian of the Seabees Museum, the staff of the Academy of Motion Pictures Arts and Sciences Library and Center for Motion Picture Studies, Richard Schickel, Bob Strauss, Ted Elrick, the National Archives, Kit Parker Films, Jim Bretzing, and the Japanese American National Museum, Los Angeles.

MAHALO ALSO TO

Paramount Pictures, Warner Bros., Time Warner, Turner Entertainment Company, RKO Pictures, MGM, United Artists, Walt Disney Pictures, MCA Universal, Republic Pictures, and Twentieth Century Fox.

SOUTH SEAS CINEMA SOCIETY

The South Seas Cinema Society is a Honolulu-based film society dedicated to celebrating, honoring, perpetuating, and enjoying movies/TV about Hawai'i and the Pacific Islands. In its efforts to raise awareness about, preserve, and present Pacific pictures, the South Seas Cinema Society has held film festivals at venues such as the Honolulu Academy of Arts, contributed to books such as *Made In Paradise, Hollywood's Films of Hawai'i and the South Seas*, and holds monthly meetings/screenings on O'ahu, often in collaboration with Long's Audio Video. The Society was founded in 1989 by Matt Locey (President), an assistant director on many feature film and TV productions; Robert C. Schmitt (Historian), author of the trendsetting *Hawaii in the Movies* and the former State of Hawai'i Statistician; DeSoto Brown (Vice President), collector par excellence of 20th-century Hawai'i ephemera, Poly-Pop Culture-ologist, and Bishop Museum

archivist of moving images; and Ed Rampell (Minister of Information). Walter Lord and Gordon W. Prange proved to be invaluable library sources.

PEARL HARBOR USS *ARIZONA* MEMORIAL

The National Park Service and, in particular, Daniel A. Martinez, Historian, USS *Arizona* Memorial.

This book would not have been possible without the unflagging support and love of Alma Rampell.

The staff of Eddie Brandt's Saturday Matinée—which has L.A.'s most extensive collection of rare, vintage videos—was extremely helpful, as were many of their film-fan customers, who, out of love for the art, selflessly gave unsolicited help and guidance. One such customer, writer/director Fletcher Rhoden of Mighty One Productions, committed a random act of kindness, mailing (at his own expense) a complimentary copy of the documentary *USS Arizona, The Life & Death of a Lady.*

Bennett Hymer, who had the faith and vision to do it again!

Luis I. Reyes made an invaluable contribution and put up with Ed Rampell.

ALOHA TO THE UNFORGOTTEN

Manhattan's Hunter College's Cinema Department and the beloved professors—especially Chairman Joel Zucker, Ken Roberts, Dick Tomkins, and Jiri Weiss—who hopefully taught their movie-maniac student well.

Richard and Arlene Rampell, who told their *niele* little boy every time they passed a movie marquee that *Three Blind Mice and a Rat Like You* was playing, and who later bought him a Super 8mm movie camera when he told them he wanted to major in cinema. See, folks—he finally got a job!!!

Mahalo Nui Loa!

Douglas Peebles

REMEMBERING PEARL HARBOR

REMEMBERING
PEARL HARBOR

INFAMY, INFIDELS, INVISIBILITY, INFIDELITY, INFINITY, AND INNOCENCE LOST

By Ed Rampell

INFAMY

SIXTY YEARS LATER, oil from the USS *Arizona* still trickles into the waters of Pearl Harbor, like blood flowing from a wound never healed. Images of that fateful early Sunday morning air raid on December 7, 1941 have left an eternal indelible impression on the collective psyche:

Out at sea, Imperial pilots don Hachimaki headbands; American servicemen rest; flyers pray at seaborne Shinto shrines; men in uniform go to church; Admiral Heihachiro Togo's historic Z battle flag from the Russo-Japanese War is raised on the Japanese carrier *Akagi*; Hawaiian music plays on the radio; flyers bolt towards their fighters and bombers; the State Department prepares to receive the Emperor's envoys in Washington; Zeros zoom off carrier decks at dawn; a sleepy, unsuspecting tropical isle; Japanese sailors wildly wave caps; soldiers attend an outdoor religious service at Kāneʻohe; the sun rises, looking like a Japanese flag; wings with rising-sun insignias soar over Oʻahu; unconcerned Hawaiʻi residents hardly heed the warplanes overhead; fighters varoom near Kolekole

Pass; a band plays "The Star-Spangled Banner" on the *Nevada*, moored at Battleship Row; Zeros fly above sugar cane and pineapple fields; sailors toss a baseball; sudden strafing; surprised swabbies hit the deck; high-altitude bombers drop their payloads; "all quarters" sounds at Pearl Harbor; U.S. planes, neatly lined up wingtip-to-wingtip, demolished at Hickam; "AIR RAID PEARL HARBOR, THIS IS NOT A DRILL!"; torpedoes career into battleships; seamen abandon ship, jumping into the harbor; raging fires engulf ships, planes, and even the water; half-dressed enlisted men dash towards battle stations; red meatballs; explosions everywhere; a black mess attendant fires a machine gun skyward; triumphant, smiling samurai pilots give each other thumbs up; burning hangars; ack-ack; dogfights; stretcher-bearers carry wounded; "Banzai!" cheers; the USS *Oklahoma* capsizes; confusion; the USS *Arizona* explodes; more than 1,100 sailors are killed as a 1,000-foot smoking fireball shoots skyward; carnage; black smoke billowing everywhere like massive cumulus clouds;

Crumpled and toppling, the battleship *Arizona* belches smoke after the surprise Japanese attack on Pearl Harbor, Hawaiʻi, on December 7, 1941.

corpses; and before FDR rallies a troubled nation, denouncing the date that will live in infamy and asking Congress to declare war, perhaps the most enduring image of all: Burt Lancaster majestically rushes onto an army barracks rooftop firing an automatic weapon, jubilantly shooting a Zero down...

PEARL HARBOR AND THE PERSISTENCE OF MOVIE MEMORY

These mental pictures linger long after the last smoke has faded away from Pearl Harbor for several reasons. For one thing, the air offensive plunged the United States into the global conflagration then sweeping the world. America's entry into WWII irrevocably changed for all time the course of this country's destiny, as well as that of Japan, Hawai'i, and probably all other nations. The way the Imperial attack was carried out also continues to reverberate in the mass mind. But one other essential ingredient ensures the fateful events of December 7, 1941 will never be forgotten.

Pearl Harbor is arguably the most filmed battle in the history of America—if not of the whole world (the USS *Arizona* remains the most-visited destination in Hawai'i). Several factors explain why it was—and continues to be—so filmed. Not least among them is the fact that by sheer coincidence, Fox Movietone cameraman Al Brick—who was lensing background shots for the Hollywood feature film *To the Shores of Tripoli*—was actually on location in Pearl during the surprise attack, and filmed a sort of Pearl Harbor equivalent to the Zapruder Film (8mm footage of the Kennedy assassination) in the assault's immediate aftermath. Two military men actually filmed the attack itself. As film historian Thomas Doherty notes in his *Projections of War, Hollywood, American Culture, And World War II*: "The symbiosis between the war and the newsreels began literally from day one."

While Brick's presence at Pearl seems to be singular luck, the Japanese who planned the surprise assault obviously had prior knowledge, and prepared for it as a mass media experience. Imperial warships and planes were armed with cameras, in order to record and screen the battle for the Greater East Asia Co-Prosperity Sphere. Flight Commander Mitsuo Fuchida—who sent the *Tora! Tora! Tora!* signal—had a camera mounted in his plane. But the Japanese film eventually fell into Allied hands, and U.S. documentaries frequently note that Pearl Harbor footage (especially exciting aerial sequences) are derived from captured Tokyo reels. So, cinematically speaking, WWII started off with a bang for America.

The fact that there's actual footage of the attack has helped to indelibly stamp Pearl images in the public's mind. However, as a trained film historian and critic, I must quickly note here that motion pictures—features and documentaries—are hardly content-neutral. Even those cameras perched atop traffic lights on city streets or inside banks are more than mere recording devices, and have points of view. Human beings not only designed them, but chose the camera angles they shoot at. Their purposes—to inform news viewers about rush-hour traffic, or assist police in apprehending speeders or bank robbers—belie the simplistic notion of video vérité. Movies are always a matter of not just recorded reality, but of a perception of that reality.

Where do films come from? Are they blown by the trade winds? Do they flow from the waves? Do they explode out of volcanoes? No—movies are a mass medium typically created by sizable casts and crews and intended for viewing by far larger audiences. When it comes to cinema, there's no such thing as art for art's sake (unless you mean Arthur Penn). Movies are made by human beings interacting with other human beings.

Moreover, movies not only express the consciousness of filmmakers and audiences, but are also emanations of what Jung called the "collective unconscious." Features and documentaries are cultural artifacts that tell us about the people being portrayed, as well as those doing the depicting. Movies reveal the social attitudes of their creators, audiences, financiers, societies, and times—about race, sex, class, gender, war, peace and more.

In this motion picture history book, we look at the feature films, documentaries, and TV programs about Pearl Harbor—the actual sneak attack, as well as the Naval base itself. We focus on Hollywood movies, although we also critique some of Japan's pictures about its *bushido* blitz of O'ahu. We also review some films dealing with Imperial attacks on other places across the International Date Line, the same day Tokyo bombed Pearl Harbor—December 8, 1941. And we include some relevant homefront pics.

Our approach as cinema historians will vary from sociological to lighthearted, psychological,

entertaining, or political. In this chapter in particular, and to a certain extent throughout this book, this sub-category of the South Seas Cinema genre will be put in context and its underlying themes analyzed, to try and understand what these moving images tell us: about America, Japan, Pearl Harbor, Hawai'i, our anxieties, our hopes, what bedevils us, our better angels, and more.

Cinema may be a looking glass that reflects society's values, fears, etc., but at the same time, as Pop Culture-ologists (to coin a phrase), we never lose sight of the fact that with the possible exception of documentaries, we're dealing with a mass entertainment medium. As such, in addition to their patriotism, drama, and social implications, many Pearl pictures are good fun. We enjoyed re-seeing most of these old friends, and hope you'll get a kick out of revisiting them, too. It's hard not to laugh watching Jerry Lewis' hijinks as an O'ahu-stationed sword-dancing swabbie in 1951's *Sailor Beware*, or flyer John Belushi's bringing the war home to Hollywood Boulevard in 1979's *1941*. The only job better than getting paid to watch movies is making them!

INFIDELS: THE FACELESS ENEMY AND SCREEN STEREOTYPES

It's interesting to note that there's not a single significant American character of consequence in either of the Japanese films *Imperial Navy* or *I Bombed Pearl Harbor*. In Costa-Gavras' 1969 *Z*, faces of policemen beating demonstrators are never seen, just as Teutonic knights in Eisenstein's

Van Johnson (left) and members of the all-Nisei 442nd in a scene from *Go For Broke*.

Alexander Nevsky (shot shortly before Nazis invaded the USSR) are obscured by helmets. Rendering the "enemy" faceless—especially a foreign one—serves not only to deprive him of individuality and his identity, but to deny his essential humanity. Not surprisingly, the Japanese are similarly vilified in most American depictions of the attack.

Yet when enemy characters are included in most Pearl pics, newsreels and documentaries, ethnic stereotypes of the Japanese are rampant. Racial slurs have been used as recently as 2001's ABC-TV remake of *South Pacific*, which repeatedly used the pejorative "Jap." This leads to a disclaimer:

As Spike Lee said regarding 2000's *Bamboozled* (about minstrel and other images caricaturing blacks), celluloid stereotypes are harmful and hurt people. The creators of this book fully realize and recognize this fact, but feel deleting and/or sugarcoating ethnic epithets and accounts of culturally insensitive depictions would not only be cinematic censorship, but would undermine the cause of examining, exposing, and debunking racial profiling onscreen. Therefore, at the risk of unintentionally offending anyone, unlike wartime censors (on both sides), we won't cut racist references, and apologize in advance if any reader is in any way harmed by words or images that are culturally incorrect. These tropes are presented not to titillate, but to educate—because they existed. As Donald Bogle, author of the brilliant *Toms, Coons, Mulattoes, Mammies, & Bucks, An Interpretive History of Blacks in American Films*, said at a February 2001 reading in L.A., it's very important to discuss screen stereotypes.

In most U.S. Pearl pictures, Imperial Japanese are frequently depicted as modern-day samurai. It's not that these Asian pilots, soldiers, etc., are exactly portrayed as less than human. In 1970's *Tora! Tora! Tora!*, TV's *Pearl*, and other films, Admiral Yamamoto is depicted as a brilliant strategist. Japanese, and other Asians, are frequently endowed with superior cunning, which triggered a rash of proto-Bondian espionage/detective films (the pre war characters Fu Manchu, Emperor Ming the Merciless, Mr. Moto, and Charlie Chan all fall into this crafty category). So, it's not necessarily a matter of being represented as inferior to humans (i.e., white Americans), but rather as something other than human.

When the Japanese struck Pearl Harbor, they struck a nerve, an underlying anxiety in America's

psyche, which predates Columbus and goes at
least as far back as Medieval Europe. Christianity's
obsession with "infidels" led to the Crusades and
the Inquisition. Centuries later, it fed into
America's racial reflex response to Tokyo and
AJAs. Instead of condemning Imperial Japan on
the basis of its system, and arguing democracy is
better for the masses of people than fascism, most
Hollywood movies resorted to racial arguments.

History, it's said, is written by the victors.
For this reason, American films are generally
made for audiences of the dominant majority
culture, created by white filmmakers and
financed by whites. Much like the silly or
menacing blackface characters that defiled
African-Americans in early twentieth century
films, Asians from Charlie Chan to Imperial
militarists were often depicted in "yellowface."
A publicity account regarding James Cagney's
1945 *Blood on the Sun* is titled *Four Hours To
Make A Jap*, and recounts how Tinseltown makeup artists transformed "white Caucasian actors
in[to] the roles of Colonel Hideki Tojo" and
other imperialists.

Not surprisingly, post-war Japanese have a
different take on Pearl Harbor. In features such
as *Imperial Navy*, the one-dimensional quality of
Hollywood's "Japs" is rounded out. A homefront
story about a mother's love, and the girl back
home, humanizes the Japanese Naval officers.

INVISIBILITY

In the documentary *The Celluloid Closet*, Harvey
Fierstein—the actor/playwright of 1988's *Torch Song
Trilogy*—said it was better for gays to be
misrepresented in Hollywood flicks as swishy than
for them to not appear at all. Fierstein said that
even negative stereotypes acknowledge a group's
existence, which he argued is better than being
completely ignored, as if one doesn't exist at all.

Although the attack takes place in their Islands,
indigenous people and other locals are often absent
from Pearl Harbor movies. There's no significant
character born and raised on Oʻahu in all of 1953's
From Here to Eternity, nor in most Pearl pictures.
Watching coming attractions for 2001's *Pearl
Harbor*, one ponders: were there any Hawaiians or
other locals on Oʻahu on December 7, 1941?

One reason for this misconception is that most
Tinseltown filmmakers, like their audiences, are not
local. Film is a mass entertainment medium
requiring wide audiences to become profitable, and
in America, there are fewer Hawaiians than
Indians—and look how Hollywood treated them.

When locals do appear, it's often to serve the
all-important Lord Jim military and government
characters—in minor parts as waitresses, caddies,
barmaids, servants, etc. Musician/actor Moe Keale
plays a cabbie who chauffeurs Midge Forrest
(Angie Dickinson) on a wild goose chase in *Pearl*
as Oʻahu burns. Moe has a memorable line of

INTRODUCTION

xv

dialogue—one of the few local speaking parts in all the Pearl pix—which is extremely apropos, considering how neurotic Midge is: "You one crazy haole!"

As most Pearl pix concentrate on Mainland actors playing military-related lead roles, little if any attention's ever paid to how the air raid affected the hundreds of thousands of civilians who, you know, kind of lived there.

Another factor contributing to turning locals into phantoms in their own home where the stories are set is that the territorial population was overwhelmingly nonwhite, including more than 140,000 persons of Japanese descent, according to Ford's *December 7th —The Movie*.

There are, however, two main exceptions to this rule relegating Islanders to insignificant roles in their own homeland. One is when locals play fifth columnists. In *December 7th*, Ford (who helmed 1949's *She Wore a Yellow Ribbon* and other Duke Wayne Indian-fighting vehicles) views AJAs with suspicion. In Howard Hawks' notoriously racist 1943 *Air Force*, Maui and O'ahu residents of Japanese origin collaborate with Tojo during the Imperial attack.

The other exception to Islander anonymity is as the significant other of an important leading character. In the Pearl Harbor category of the South Seas film genre, non-military dependent love interests are usually with two types of women. The first is hookers in the Sadie Thompson mold. But these onscreen vixens are generally continental imports, such as Donna Reed in *Eternity* and Jane Russell in Raoul Walsh's *The Revolt of Mamie Stover*. In *Pearl*, in a downtown Honolulu house of ill-repute, soldier John Zawalsky (Adam Arkin) paints a portrait of a whore (Char Fontain), and brawls with impatient customers. Of course, Hotel Street really was so full of brothels up to 1944 that prostitutes actually went on strike—and won.

The other type of Pearl partnering involves consorting with Island women. Miscegenation has long been a staple of South Seas Cinema—think of Clark Gable and his Tahitian lover, played by Hawaiian actress Mamo Clark in 1935's *Mutiny On the Bounty*. Pacific pictures minus interracial sex is like Aunt Jemima's pancakes without the syrup. And in Pearl pix, these lovers are usually women of Asian ancestry.

These affairs can sometimes be viewed as love conquering all. From Harlequin Romance novels to *Romeo and Juliet*, the love-story formula calls for formidable obstacles lovers must strive to overcome.

This is spicier when the hurdle to be cleared is an ethnic barrier—think of 1961's *West Side Story*, when Shakespeare's "what's in a name?" took on the Puerto Rican-white twist.

More cynically, East-West relationships in Pearl pictures can be viewed as perpetuating the exotic erotic syndrome fixated on geisha girl-type tropes. In *Pearl*, Naval Lt. J.G. "Doug" North (Gregg Henry) refers to Holly Nagata (Tiana Alexandra) as "Madame Butterfly." North's a military brat, reared and schooled in Hawai'i; Holly, a Nisei reporter for a Honolulu newspaper. Holly's parents oppose their interracial relationship. In 1976's *Midway*, Charlton Heston plays a high-ranking officer whose ensign son, Edward Albert, loves a Japanese woman, Christina Kokubo, who's interned.

Meanwhile, back at the homefront, in Pearl Harbor's wake, AJAs are herded en masse into internment camps. In 1990's poignant *Come See the Paradise*, Dennis Quaid falls for Little Tokyo's Tamlyn Tomita, who's ordered to the camps. Ten years later, there's a similar American boy-Japanese girl love entanglement in *Snow Falling on Cedars*.

Although Hawaiians have yet to be in a position to direct feature films, Native artists have given expression to an Islander experience of what Pearl Harbor means to them. Novelist Kiana Davenport vividly describes the attack from a local perspective in her novels *Shark Dialogues* and *Song of the Exile*. Composer Leo Akana gives voice to Hawaiians in her *Pearl Harbor Blues*, performed by the Peter Moon Band. AJA writer Jon Shirota describes the December 7, 1941 events in his witty 1966 novel *Lucky Come Hawai'i*—a local companion piece to *Eternity*, written with the help of a James Jones-Lowney Handy grant—and returns to the war's impact on Islanders in his play *Leilani's Hibiscus*, about a doomed love affair between a Hawaiian and an Okinawan.

INFIDELITY AS PEARL HARBOR METAPHOR

In the Polynesian night silence, waves crash on the swimsuited Burt Lancaster and Deborah Kerr, who are caressing and embracing prone on the beach at southeast O'ahu's Halona Cove in 1953's *From Here to Eternity*. Kerr breathlessly moans magic words all lovers yearn to hear: "I never knew it could be like this!" It's arguably the most romantic scene in movie history.

The stirring sequence is certainly one of filmdom's most imitated (though never surpassed), providing fodder for TV comics such as Sid Caesar and Imogene Coca, and former Oʻahu resident Carol Burnett. The *Eternity* scene inspired dramas, too—most notably another black-and-white tryst on an Oʻahu beach in 1965's *In Harm's Way*.

But most viewers forget why the *Eternity* lovers dally at the Blowhole beach in the dead of night. Lancaster plays Sgt. Milton Warden, while Kerr portrays Karen Holmes—the wife of Warden's Commanding Officer, Major Holmes. The buxom blonde O'Brian makes love to near Makapuʻu in *In Harm's Way* is married to Naval officer Paul Eddington (Kirk Douglas). Later, Eddington in turn has relations with a Navy nurse—who's engaged to the son of his best friend and C.O., Rear Admiral Rock Torrey (John Wayne).

In *Winds of War* and its sequel *War and Remembrance*, Naval officer Pug Henry is married to Rhoda Henry; both cheat on each other: she with his close friend Palmer. In *Eternity*, Prewitt (Montgomery Clift) must compete with other G.I. Johns for his girlfriend Alma, a prostitute calling herself "Lorene." In *Pearl*, Angie Dickinson makes love to her high-ranking husband's men. In *Pearl Harbor*, Danny (Josh Hartnett) proceeds to woo Evelyn (Kate Beckinsale), his best friend Rafe's (Ben Affleck) girl, after Rafe is believed to be killed in battle.

Thus, starting with 1953's *Eternity*, infidelity has been used as a metaphor for the Imperial sneak attack on Pearl Harbor. "Sneaking around," of course, is a commonly used term describing sexual disloyalty. Unsuspecting spouses and partners (usually males) are betrayed by those expected to be closest to them. Adultery breaks a sacred Judeo-Christian commandment and bond of trust. In the case of *Eternity* and *Pearl*, commanding officers are betrayed by lower-ranking soldiers. Unfaithful lovers unconsciously symbolize Japanese invaders, who conspire and commit treachery—on the morning of a Sunday, no less, the Christian day of rest. As narrator Eric Sevareid says in the documentary *America Goes to War*: "The surprise attack on Pearl Harbor would become synonymous with treachery."

During the war years themselves, the issue of trustworthiness recurs in espionage flicks. *Secret Agent of Japan* (1942) was perhaps the first American feature dealing with WWII released after Pearl Harbor. Shanghai nightclub owner Preston

Foster, a Yank on the lam from U.S. law, is attracted to beautiful Lynn Bari—but is she a spy? And is the helpful Asian played by Sen Young (later *Bonanza*'s Hop Sing) friend or foe? In 1945's *Blood on the Sun*, James Cagney is a hardboiled newspaperman in pre-Pearl Tokyo tortured by indecision: can he trust the beautiful Eurasian double agent played by Sylvia Sydney? Humphrey Bogart has the same problem with shipmates in 1942's *Across the Pacific*—can he trust Nisei passenger Sen Young and Mary Astor, whom he's falling for in this tale about a Japanese raid on the Panama Canal? In the wake of December 7, these films ask: who will stab us in the back and whom can we trust?

Obsession with betrayal and trust is also projected into numerous films questioning the loyalty of those in America with "Oriental" ancestry. Sen Young's loyalty in *Secret Agent of Japan* and *Across the Pacific* depends, predictably, on whether he portrays Chinese or Japanese characters. In 1942's *To the Shores of Tripoli*, at a patriotic Marine march, an Asian man wears a sign proclaiming "Me Chinese," and waves Old Glory, as a white woman stares at him incredulously. While an Asian could "clear" himself by establishing his bona fides as a non-Japanese, the shadow of suspicion fell hardest on those who actually were of Japanese heritage. They're often portrayed as traitorous saboteurs in the heat-of-the-moment Hollywood pics made during the war, such as *Air Force*. Unlike white soldiers who have nothing to prove, Americans of Japanese ancestry must prove their loyalty in a segregated U.S. Army unit, the Fighting 442nd, in 1951's *Go For Broke!* Or they're interned victims in the postwar *Come See the Paradise*.

Of course, the issue of trust is amplified and intensified when it takes on a sexual dimension. Besides infidelity, other forms of illicit sex violate bourgeois morality and are unconscious projections of what President Roosevelt dubbed "a date which shall live in infamy." *Pearl*'s handsome soldier, the Finger, is accused of homosexuality—ironically, the man he cuckolds, Colonel Forrest, calls him "that homo." Interracial love, which recurs in Pearl pics, is also tabu. Prostitution, by Mamie, Lorene, etc., defiles intimacy, reducing it to mere commerce. In Woody Allen's 1987 *Radio Days*, set in the early 1940s, Mia Farrow plays a bimbo who sells more than cigarettes at a swanky Manhattan nightclub in order to sleep her way to broadcasting stardom.

Pearl's madam observes: "It's my business serving the military."

But a more potent symbol of "immoral" sex outside the confines of church-sanctioned marriage and for strictly procreative purposes is rape. America widely perceived that her innocence was violated by the Pearl Harbor surprise attack. An act of force transgressed American purity. In *In Harm's Way*, Douglas rapes the Navy nurse Annie (Jill Hayworth). Van Heflin rapes a young Filipina in *Cry of Battle*, after her family has taken him and MacArthur into their nipa hut to hide them from the Japanese.

In keeping with the Judeo-Christian ethos of a vengeful, all-seeing god, these dastardly deeds don't go unpunished. In *In Harm's Way*, O'Brian pays for his sandy romp with Eddington's wife: they awake outdoors and unprotected on December 7, 1941 to be mowed down by Zeros. Eddington's wife's infidelity triggers erratic behavior in the Naval officer. Later, when his rape results in Annie's pregnancy, she commits suicide. Finding out she was the fiancée of his best friend's son, Douglas seeks redemption by commandeering a plane for a suicide mission, so the island-hopping campaign will succeed. Announcement of the Pearl Harbor sneak attack preempts Mia Farrow's long-sought-after debut on national radio. And of course, in *Pearl Harbor*, Danny must pay for his disloyalty to Rafe, and die for his transgression.

Verily, the wicked are smote by the righteous—just as America will exact revenge from the Land of the Rising Sun, and make Tokyo pay dearly for its infamous perfidy!

FROM ZERO TO INFINITY

Based on and/or dealing with the same singular historical event, Pearl pictures inevitably use recurring images and themes with varying degrees of accuracy and authenticity. (The important issue of fact versus fiction is covered case-by-case in movie reviews following this section of the book). The classic cliches of Pearl Harbor, repeated in many documentaries and features, include:

Americans receive news of the attack via the 1940s' most prevalent means of mass communications, the radio. In the back seat of a cab with his girlfriend, John Payne, who has just returned to civilian life in *To the Shores of Tripoli*, takes a just-purchased radio out of a box and turns it on. Turning the dial he hears the fateful news.

Pearl's Holly Nagata and Lt. Doug North are beachside when they play a car radio and hear the news flash. *The Fighting Sullivans* (1944) hear the news at home over the radio. Woody Allen's droll *Radio Days* sends up this well-worn scene by having it take place in a broadcast studio.

FDR's stirring post-Pearl speech to Congress is heard as a broadcast, glimpsed as a newsreel, or reenacted. It opens *I Bombed Pearl Harbor*, the Toho Company's 1961 feature starring Toshiro Mifune, as a voice-over that's heard as the waves carrying the Imperial task force are seen. Jon Voight as Roosevelt, steel leg braces and all, delivers the historic "date which shall live in infamy" address in *Pearl Harbor*.

Admiral Yamamoto's disappointment at learning the Imperial task force failed to deliver the decisive blow to U.S. Naval forces, in particular because American aircraft carriers were away from Pearl on December 7, is found in the Japanese-made *Admiral Yamamoto*, *I Bombed Pearl Harbor*, and *Imperial Navy*, as well as the U.S.-Japan coproduction *Tora! Tora! Tora!*, and *The Gallant Hours*. His regrets (sans carrier references) are also found in *Pearl* and *Pearl Harbor*.

Zooming Zeros bursting out of the clouds strafing, bombing, and torpedoing Hawai'i, and fanatical warriors screaming "Banzai!", are depicted in more films than this historian cares to remember. But the most oft-repeated cliché involves the petty—and sometimes steamy—personal lives of O'ahu's officers, enlisted men, and civilians, which are rudely interrupted by the attack.

INNOCENCE LOST

December 7, 1941 is a defining moment in American history. It is, perhaps, the second most famous date in U.S. history (after July 4, 1776). But what exactly does it define?

Coming attractions for 2001's *Pearl Harbor* proclaim: "It was the end of innocence…" This is a popular refrain, a leitmotif recurring even 60 years after that fateful Sunday morning in Hawai'i. In *Pearl*, after the bombs have fallen, the philosophical Southerner Captain Lanford raises a toast and says: "Here's to the end of personal choice… I know as suddenly as if a huge blade had dropped and cut my past off from my future that from this moment forward, I don't control tomorrow, or any of the tomorrows I may have left until God knows when."

down instead of U.S. planes—a begoggled Reagan plays a hotshot Pacific-theatre pilot. Although the future President actually fought the war in Culver City, to his credit, the actor enlisted in the Army and served in a propaganda function. The opening credits of *Jap Zero* read: "The U.S. Government presents a Product of the First Motion Picture Unit Army Air Force. Released by the Office of War Information Bureau of Motion Pictures."

Furthermore, Hollywood features were themselves subject to, and vehicles of, U.S. propaganda. It's common for movies to cite assistance from the armed forces; the end credits of 1934's *Here Comes the Navy* (in which James Cagney is a swabbie aboard the USS *Arizona*) acknowledge U.S. Navy assistance. Twenty-six years later, the end credits of *The Gallant Hours* (a biopic starring Cagney as Admiral Halsey) offer: "Sincere appreciation for the cooperation extended by the United States Department of Defense and most specifically, by the United States Navy and Marine Corps." Abbot and Costello's 1941 *In the Navy* is dedicated to the San Diego and San Pedro USN bases, officers, and enlisted personnel "in grateful appreciation for their invaluable cooperation." *Pearl*'s profuse credits expressing gratitude to the U.S. government and DOD for cooperation explicitly thank the military's "Public Affairs Office."

Another staple of WWII flicks are credits citing retired or active duty servicemen as "technical advisers." *Run Silent* is not only based on a Naval Commander's novel, but cites a Rear Admiral as technical adviser. *The Winds of War* gives this credit to Captain Bill Graves, USN Retired.

DOD cooperation and use of technical advisers not only provide an aura of authenticity and accuracy, but also arguably orthodoxy, making sure filmmakers don't stray off the proverbial reservation. Directors and others who don't adhere to the Pentagon party line are unlikely to receive Defense Department support. The U.S. military refused to cooperate with Francis Ford Coppola vis-à-vis his 1979 anti-Vietnam War pic *Apocalypse Now*, and Coppola resorted to renting helicopters from Ferdinand Marcos—which, ironically, were frequently unavailable as the Philippines military battled its own insurgency.

It is also worth noting that Hollywood's Production Code—industry self-regulation designed to preempt overt government censorship of motion pictures—restricted film content, such as subversive, anti-patriotic messages. First Amendment guarantees did not automatically apply to early-1940s movies.

Shooting on location at the O'ahu installation, *Pearl Harbor* received Defense Department authorization and cooperation, and it's possible that CINCPAC had some form of script review, if not approval—though not exactly final cut. But in any case, why did Disney spend a king's ransom on an oft-filmed WWII saga, which the Pentagon so willingly cooperated with? Of course, December 7, 2001, marks the 60th anniversary of that infamous date. During the 50th anniversary, Twentieth Century Fox marked the occasion by re-releasing 10 Pearl Harbor and WWII pics on video as a set, including *Tora! Tora! Tora!*

In recent years, Computer Generated Images and other high-tech wizardry have vastly improved cinematic special effects. *Pearl Harbor* reportedly has 180 digital effects. Furthermore, as the Production Code is gone with the trade winds, and films now have the Constitution's free speech protections, movies today are more graphic and candid than ever. Hence, the big screen is taking another look at historic battles, enhancing film realism with technical innovations and artistic liberty. The opening D-Day battle sequence in 1998's *Saving Private Ryan* is far bloodier than 1962's black-and-white *The Longest Day*. Ditto for 1998's *The Thin Red Line* compared to 1943's *Guadalcanal Diary*. The Mel Gibson epics *Braveheart* (1995—written by *P.H.* screenwriter Randall Wallace) and *The Patriot* (2000) are also part of this trend, as are 2001's *Pearl Harbor* and *Enemy at the Gates*, a visceral, breathtaking epic about the Battle of Stalingrad.

Pearl Harbor also dovetails into the disaster genre. Since the late 1990s, Hollywood has filled screens with larger-than-life volcanic eruptions, twisters, earthquakes, extraterrestrial invasions, floods, asteroid collisions, dinosaurs, etc. Like the Y2K hysteria, these movies express an underlying Biblical anxiety about the endtime as we enter a new millennium. Several pictures explicitly deal with apocalyptic New Testament themes, such as Arnold Schwarzenegger's *End of Days*.

In a recent American Movies Classic documentary on disaster films, Pearl Harbor is almost the only battle covered. Pearl, of course, was an unmitigated debacle, costing more than 2,000 lives. It also flung America into the maelstrom of the most apocalyptic war ever, from the concentration camps to Hiroshima and Nagasaki.

Given all of the above, another piece of historic fiction in 2000 may shed light on why Hollywood is not only releasing what is the latest in a long line of Pearl pictures, but lavishing so much moolah and hoopla on it, with DOD support. *Thirteen Days* is an intense drama about the 1962 Cuban Missile Crisis, detailing how the Soviets deployed nuclear missiles 90 miles from Florida, bringing the world to the brink of thermonuclear war between East and West.

Pearl Harbor—the movie, the attack, the base—all deal with the recurring theme of backstabbing, of being taken by surprise. Why did these two films appear back to back?

Both are, of course, movies with points of view. Like *Thirteen Days, Pearl Harbor* rings alarm bells about sneak attacks and not being prepared. Terrorism—whether by extremist factions such as Bin-Laden's alleged Afghan-based operation or the state-sponsored variety by so-called rogue states like Libya—is still perceived as an unresolved problem for Washington (as well as other countries). The terrorist attack on the USS *Cole* at Aden in 2000 blew a gaping hole in a warship and took Navy lives. That surprise attack caused widespread questioning not only about perceived terrorist threats, but military preparedness and procedures, too. In February 2001, a nuclear-powered U.S. submarine stationed at Pearl crashed into a Japanese fishing vessel during a surfacing exercise. This was followed by the collision of two military helicopters. Sixteen people were killed in the two accidents, raising more questions about military preparedness, training, and judgment. Later that month, a top FBI counterintelligence officer was charged with being a double agent, and our leaders promptly reminded us that the world's still a very VERY unsafe place (even 10 years after we won the Cold War).

But in addition to terrorist anxieties, *Thirteen Days* and *Pearl Harbor* tap into another underlying issue. Both Al Gore and George W. Bush ran for president favoring a National Missile Defense (NMD) program. Advocates contend this will provide America (and some allies) with a nuclear shield that'll prevent enemy warheads from reaching U.S. shores. But domestic and foreign opponents (including Russia, China, and most allies) condemn this latest version of Reagan's "Star Wars" anti-missile scheme as too expensive and a multi-billion-dollar defense contractor boondoggle. Critics also claim the antiballistic missile system will ignite a new arms race and abrogate existing arms control treaties. Furthermore, dissidents maintain that since the Cold War's end, there's no longer an enemy or need requiring deployment of an NMD that, they assert, is technologically impossible, and won't work anyway. No matter what the truth is, National Missile Defense is a tough sell.

Enter Hollywood. With their messages about never again being caught with your pants down, *Thirteen Days* and *Pearl Harbor* may be unconscious projections of the proposed National Missile Defense, which proponents insist will protect the United States from surprise nuclear attack.

It's also intriguing to note that the May 21, 2001 world premiere of *Pearl Harbor* on a U.S. aircraft carrier at Pearl came hard on the heels of the standoff between the People's Republic of China and the United States following the early-spring midair collision of a Chinese fighter jet and a U.S. spy plane, which made an emergency landing on Chinese territory. *Pearl Harbor* may be an unconscious premonition and projection of yet another Asian-versus-American clash in the 21st century.

REMEMBERING PEARL HARBOR MOVIES

Be that as it may, the reportedly $165-million Disney feature, plus approximately nine new documentaries about the attack, will play a vital role in perpetuating the Pearl Harbor legacy. As the numbers of the Greatest Generation who fought during WWII dwindle, these films will serve to raise the consciousness of younger generations about their heroic sacrifice, what they fought against, and for.

World War II was the U.S. military's most gallant hour and the quintessential Good Fight. Those who fell at Pearl, Hickam, Wheeler, Kāneʻohe, Schofield, etc.—2,403 dead and 1,178 wounded sailors, soldiers, Marines, civilians, and locals—were the first victims of fascist aggression on U.S. territory. But the ultimate triumph over fascism means their sacrifice was not in vain. With this book, we honor all the fallen and those still with us. If not for you, we might have been born slaves—or perhaps not at all… We salute you and wish you all the warmest of aloha. We gratefully say from the depths of our souls: mahalo nui loa for your role in saving the younger generations from the terrors of fascism and ensuring we're freer and far better off than we would have been without your cherished, glorious sacrifices.

Long after the last drop of the USS *Arizona's* oil has wept into its nearby waters, movies—new and old—about that day of infamy, infidels, infidelity, invisibility, infinity, and innocence lost will make sure the world forever remembers Pearl Harbor.

Dennis Oda

Members of the *Pearl Harbor* cast, including (from left to right) Cuba Gooding, Jr., Josh Hartnett and Ben Affleck, join an actual Pearl Harbor survivor in a show of respect at the USS *Arizona* Memorial.

CHAPTER 1
Conspiracy Films

CONSPIRACY FILMS

CONSPIRACY THEORIES RELATING to the Pearl Harbor sneak attack abound. After Admiral Yamamoto discovers, much to his chagrin, that the U.S. carriers escaped the destruction, the narrator of the Japanese feature *Imperial Navy* states: "America was united as never before in its desire to avenge Pearl Harbor. There were even suggestions that President Roosevelt himself deliberately let Pearl Harbor happen to motivate the American people to wage a war." This conspiracy theory is repeated in Gore Vidal's 2000 novel *The Golden Age*, and in *Pearl Harbor*, intelligence sources warn FDR the Naval installation is a target. But in most Pearl features (especially Tinseltown's), it is the Japanese who are seen as conspiratorial.

There's something strangely reassuring about conspiracy theories—they lend causality and reason to events which could otherwise be viewed as random happenstance. And they can explain away one's own shortcomings by projecting the causes of disasters on others. In the same way that Hitler blamed the Jews for causing Germany to lose WWI (and for every other German ailment) U.S. forces were so thoroughly routed at Pearl not because of their lackadaisical ineptitude, but because of the perfidy of both the external enemy and the enemy within. Hollywood's wartime agitprop obsessed over fifth-column sabotage and subterfuge.

In 1979's *Pearl*, ensconced in Iolani Palace, Colonel North orders Shinto priests rounded up, and rants about Imperial conspiracies. The racist quotes an old Hawaiian proverb—"The canoe is not swamped by the outside wave, but by the inside wave"—and insists that the Japanese migration to Hawai'i, which began in the 19th century, was part of a grand plan of conquest. "Why are so many here? They were planning, waiting for this very moment!" Adding that the AJAs have concealed weapons, Dennis Weaver almost foams at the mouth during this histrionic scene, for which the "yellow peril" is the subtext.

Of course, Commander Minoru Genda and company did meticulously plan the raid, and were assisted by espionage activities in Hawai'i, notably by a Naval Intelligence officer. But wide-scale sabotage, or even insurrection, never occurred. Proponents of the internment camps might argue this was due to diligent preemptive action by an alert government, but this belief is belied by the fact that in Hawai'i, the place with the heaviest concentration of AJAs, they were not put into detention camps. They may have committed treason onscreen—notably in *Air Force*—but not off.

Indeed, Hawai'i's war effort depended on the overwhelmingly loyal AJA labor force, and the Fighting 442nd became the Army's most decorated regiment.

SECRET AGENT OF JAPAN

Twentieth Century Fox, 1942

Director: Irving Pichel

Screenwriter: John Larkin

Producer: Sol M. Wurtzel

Cast: Preston Foster, Lynn Bari, Noel Madison, Sen Yung

According to American Movies Classics, the Hollywood trade press called *Secret Agent of Japan* "the war's first inside story to reach the screen." This, plus the flick's exciting conclusion, redeem an otherwise creaky, melodramatic script full of cloak-and-dagger flourishes (such as a switch of cigarettes bearing secret messages). Leading man Preston Foster is an American abroad who's on the lam from U.S. justice (wrongfully accused of grand larceny), uses the alias "Roy Bonnell," pretends he's a Swiss national, and is only out for himself. Bonnell runs a nightclub catering to expats in late 1941 Shanghai. The Dixie's international clientele includes American oil sellers, who denounce FDR's oil embargo against Japan at the bar, plus nazi and Imperial agents. Sen Yung plays a helpful Asian called Joey who often helps Bonnell escape from jams, and Lynn Bari's a mystery woman named Kay Murdoch who poses as a buyer of jade.

Romance inevitably ensues between the rugged Bonnell and shapely Murdoch, who reveals, "I work for British Intelligence….The Japs are pulling something on Washington; we're sure of it. But we don't know the final move." A brief broadcasting scene reprises radio sequences often found in Pearl pics. But as this takes place shortly before December 7, it's not FDR on the air, but a pro-Allies announcer skeptical about Japanese expansionism and motives in the Pacific Rim. Like many Pearl pix, the radio comments on the meetings between Imperial envoy Admiral Saburo Kurusu and Japan's Ambassador to the U.S. Admiral Kichisaburo Nomura with Secretary of State Cordell Hull. "There's more than meets the eye in the resumption of the Washington conference after it broke down," warns the presenter.

In *Secret Agent of Japan*, jade plays the role of what Hitchcock calls the McGuffin, a convenient plot device that moves the story along. The characters really search for a code letter which, Imperial spy Saito (Noel Madison) tells the captured Bonnell and Murdoch, confirms that "Plan 21 has been completed. That is operation for area of Hawai'i." Saito eventually reveals that a jade "ancient sword handle contains list of Japanese agents at work in Honolulu, location of great American base. Trusted men and women prepared to direct the Japanese air raiders by short-wave transmitters, who will cut arrows in fields of sugarcane pointing way to Pearl Harbor secrets. Who will prevent your airmen from reaching their fighting planes?"

In a shoot-out, the couple escapes from the Axis spy ring to inform U.S. Naval Intelligence of the impending attack. An officer states, "Get rid of your fifth columnists and you've won half the battle." But Imperial troops—led by a uniformed Joey—burst into the office and seize the Americans and Brits and tell them: "Our airplanes bombed Pearl Harbor. American fleet is destroyed…I take charge now." Joey and his soldiers take Bonnell and Murdoch to a rural area, where they expect to be executed. But instead of a firing squad, "Joey"

reveals he's really Wu Yen, a secret agent working for Chiang Kai-Shek. Turning over the jade sword handle, he ushers them away to a plane waiting at a secret landing strip, after giving Bonnell one of the business-type cards which repeatedly crop up during the movie, stating: "Join the Chinese Army!"

This B-picture, rewritten after December 7, 1941 and released in April 1942, closely reflects the war hysteria that swept America and led to the forced relocation of most continental AJAs into internment centers. As previously noted, in *The Man Who Spied on Pearl Harbor*, Takeo Yoshikawa denied receiving support from AJAs in Hawai'i. While there may have been a few underground supporters aiding the enemy, most AJAs were loyal, and this conspiracy theory linking Zeros and saboteurs on the ground is rooted in "yellow peril" racism.

Caucasian actors like Noel Madison play Japanese characters in "yellowface." After the film's broadcast, AMC's host said: "At that time, there were very few Japanese actors working in Hollywood. Unfortunately, many were rounded up and sent to detention camps. Others still had relatives in Japan and they were afraid that if this film was shown in Japan, they might be recognized…There might be reprisals for their families." Victor Sen Yung (sometimes credited as "Young") was of Chinese ancestry, and like Keye Luke, the number-one son of Charlie Chan, he appeared in a number of 1940s flicks (although the Honolulu detective was portrayed by white thespians).

Secret Agent of Japan is a trendsetter for depicting the dissolute or self-absorbed American whose patriotism is rekindled by the war. Bonnell—whose real name, it turns out, is Carmichael—returns to the fold (even though he faces criminal charges back home) and joins the army against fascism, just as John Payne re-ups in *To the Shores of Tripoli*, another early WWII agitprop pic released the same year. *Secret Agent of Japan* may have influenced the most enduring and beloved Tinseltown wartime masterpiece, 1943's *Casablanca*. Humphrey Bogart plays a hardboiled expatriate with a past who owns a nightclub overseas, overcomes cynicism and selfishness to (re-)join the anti-fascist crusade. In addition, movies like *Secret Agent of Japan*—as the name suggests—are prototypes of the James Bond series.

LITTLE TOKYO, USA

Twentieth Century Fox, 1942

D: Otto Bower

S: George Bricker

P: Bryan Foy

Cast: Preston Foster, Brenda Joyce, Harold Huber, Don Douglas, June Duprez, Richard Loo, Sen Young

American-born Japanese businessman Ito Takimura (Huber) meets with Japanese spies in the Little Tokyo section of Los Angeles. Police detective Michael Steele (Foster) becomes suspicious of spy activities in the area. Framed by the spy ring for the murder of a Japanese woman on the evening of December 6, Steele is jailed and learns of the Japanese attack on Pearl Harbor the next morning. He escapes from jail and exposes the spy ring, bringing them to justice.

Soon after, Japanese-Americans on the West Coast are taken to internment camps, Little Tokyo becomes a ghost town and a radio commentator comments that loyal Japanese-Americans must suffer along with the disloyal in the interest of national security.

This is a blatantly racist Grade B espionage drama with clichéd characters and situations. Most of the "Japanese" characters are played by Caucasian and Chinese actors. It was partially shot on location in Los Angeles' Chinatown, as Little Tokyo was deserted by the time production began because in real life the Japanese Americans had been sent to the internment camps. Interestingly, both *Secret Agent of Japan* and *Little Tokyo, USA* share the same leading man, Preston Foster, who is also in *Wake Island* and *Guadalcanal Diary*.

ACROSS THE PACIFIC

Warner Bros., 1942

D: John Huston

S: Richard Macaulay from a story by Robert Carson

P: Jerry Wald and Jack Saper

Cast: Humphrey Bogart, Mary Astor, Sydney Greenstreet

This is a gem, an A-picture with a first-rate director, story, and cast. Huston (who joined the Army to make combat films) reprises 1941's seminal classic *The Maltese Falcon* with three of its stars, and places early film noir conventions and preoccupations into an exciting espionage drama. As in the following year's *Casablanca*, Bogie plays a character named Rick. As the film opens, an officer tears Captain Leland's sleeve at the shoulder, and Bogie appears to be disgraced, and is cashiered from the Army. He tries to enlist in the Canadian military, but the career officer, who's served at Fort Kamehameha and the Panama Canal Zone, is turned down. Rick buys a ticket from steamship office clerk Keye Luke for a Japanese freighter bound for Yokohama by way of New York, the Panama Canal, and Honolulu, with the announced intention of joining Chiang Kai-Shek's army.

Aboard the *Genoa Maru*, Rick encounters his fellow passengers Mary Astor and Sydney Greenstreet (Bogie's co-stars in *Maltese*) and Victor Sen Young. Astor plays Alberta Marlowe, who claims to be a small-town girl on a pleasure cruise. She forms a mature, kidding relationship with Rick, filled with sparkling dialogue, as they struggle with the issue of trust. Greenstreet portrays Professor Lorenz, who lectures at a university in the Philippines, where he is a citizen. Sen Young again plays an affable character named Joe who's fond of calling Leland "Ricky," a Nisei headed to Japan to help the family business.

None of the passengers are who they say they are. Joe and Lorenz are Imperial agents. Rick saves Lorenz from a Filipino assassin, and the professor tries recruiting Rick with bribes, seeking his knowledge of Canal Zone fortifications, military flights, and the like. Alberta is actually the daughter of a Panama plantation owner who's incommunicado. Monte Blue reprises his role of a drunken Yank fallen on hard times in the tropics (which he originally played in 1928's *White Shadows in the South Seas*), whose Bountiful Plantation has been taken over by Japanese laborers.

It turns out Rick is actually a U.S. undercover agent. After a shoot-out in a Canal Zone Asian movie theatre playing a Japanese comedy, Rick and Alberta are held prisoner on December 7, 1941, at the plantation, where the Japanese workers have built a secret airstrip in order to bomb that vital Pacific-Atlantic link, the Panama Canal. The *Genoa Maru*'s cargo destined for Bountiful Plantation has actually consisted of crated plane parts—and torpedoes. But as the plane prepares to take off to bomb the Canal, Rick manages to commandeer a machine-gun and

PEARL HARBOR IN THE MOVIES

Humphrey Bogart solidified his existentialist tough-guy leading-man image with his role in *Across the Pacific*, pictured here with Mary Astor, battling Japanese agents plotting to sabotage the Panama Canal. The film was directed by John Huston, who brought together many of the actors who worked on his previous hit, *The Maltese Falcon*.

Luis Reyes Collection

shoot the enemy plane, which crashes on the strip. "Any of your friends in Tokyo have trouble committing hara-kiri, those boys would be glad to help them out," Rick declares, referring to U.S. warplanes triumphantly soaring overhead.

It's unfortunate that this final sequence, in which another of the *Genoa Maru*'s inscrutable passengers is revealed to be a disguised Japanese prince, veers towards foolishness. Until then the plot has moved along smartly with intrigue and action.

In Mary Astor's autobiography she reveals that when filming began in late 1941, the movie was originally set in Hawai'i. The arrival of war in real life forced the change of settings to Panama. Sharp-eyed viewers may catch a reference to Hawai'i which escaped the rewrite: the cinema where the shoot-out occurs is called the Ewa Theatre.

Across the Pacific reflects the anxiety wartime America felt about the Japanese at home, abroad, and on the high seas. The treacherous "Joe" is specifically identified as a "Nisei," and in one shot, wears outrageous bifocals emphasized in close-up. He also flips Bogie in a martial-arts demo aboard ship. Sen Young, of course, was actually Chinese, as was Keye Luke, and most of the actors portraying

Japanese characters. Rudy Robles, however, plays the Filipino assassin, and Lee Tung Foo portrays Rick's friend Sam Wing On, a Canal Zone hotelier who's generous, helpful, and frets over Rick's safety.

BLOOD ON THE SUN

United Artists, 1945

D: Frank Lloyd

S: Lester Cole from a story by Garrett Fort

P: William and James Cagney

Cast: James Cagney, Sylvia Sidney, John Emery, Robert Armstrong

If *Across the Pacific* is vintage Bogie, *Blood on the Sun* is classic Cagney, directed by Frank Lloyd, who helmed 1935's Best Picture, *Mutiny on the Bounty*. Cagney plays Nick Condon, a Yank stationed in pre-Pearl Japan as the English-language Tokyo *Chronicle*'s hardboiled managing editor. Nick discovers the top-secret Imperial plans for global conquest and becomes Japan's public enemy number one. He must escape the Land of the Rising Sun and expose the nefarious plot. Along the way, he romances and doubts Sylvia Sydney, who portrays Iris Hilliard, a Eurasian double agent who's after the same document. In the end, it turns out that the half-Asian woman is working for the Chinese, not Japanese, and is therefore on the same side as Nick.

On the lam, Iris and Nick flee to Tokyo's docks, where they rendezvous in an over-water shack with Prince Tatsugi (Frank Puglia), a liberal member of the cabinet. The bearded elder statesman signs the document in order to authenticate it, declaring: "I would rather see Japan defeated, than triumphant under the heels of our militarists." Captain Oshima (John Halloran) shoots His Highness, and Cagney sacrifices himself, staying behind to hold off the Imperial secret police as Sylvia escapes in a prearranged boat with the document. Nick has an epic fight with the hulking Oshima; Cagney was trained in judo for six weeks to make the pitched battle as realistic as possible, according to contemporary press accounts. The training apparently paid off, as Cagney wins and somehow manages to evade the secret police and make his way to the U.S. embassy in Tokyo.

Lester Cole's fast-paced script was actually suggested by fact. According to the June 18, 1945 *Life* magazine, "The plot revolves around a bit of actual history, the Tanaka Memorial, a plan for the conquest of Manchukuo [Manchuria] which Premier Baron Tanaka supposedly submitted to the emperor in 1927." *Blood on the Sun* refers to Giichi Tanaka (John Emery in yellowface) as "an Oriental Hitler," and to the Tanaka Memorial as a Japanese *Mein Kampf* (or "My Struggle," the manifesto Hitler wrote in jail, spelling out his plans for world domination).

During the Red Scare in 1947, Cole became one of the Hollywood 10, a group of blacklisted leftist filmmakers whom the House Un-American Activities Committee accused of putting radical messages into Hollywood movies, among other things. *Blood on the Sun* is a case study of a left-wing screenwriter actually injecting progressive ideas into a Tinseltown feature, despite restrictions imposed upon dissidents by the Production Code and other censorship measures. When Iris resists Nick's advances, telling him "I'm half-Chinese," Nick jauntily replies: "I'm half-Irish, half-Norwegian." In an earlier barroom scene, Nick mocks the racial condescension of a Western correspondent by sarcastically saying: "Some of my best friends are Chinese." This flouting of the race taboo in 1940s America, where apartheid was still practiced in the South, was heady stuff. Of course Communists and other leftists, such as African-American actor Paul Robeson, were in the forefront of the civil-rights movement then. Iris is also an ardent feminist, who says her job is studying the problems of Japanese females—women's liberation is another left-wing cause.

Although *Blood* is set in the late 1920s or early 1930s, the depiction of a "liberal" Japanese politician—Prince Tatsugi—is almost unprecedented in Hollywood's wartime agitprop. While the film does have some ethnic slurs, *Blood* is notable because it shows someone born and raised in Japan resisting fascism. The Imperial system is opposed not because of race, but on the grounds of a social system, in this case, militarism. But the real kicker is what Cole surely managed to slip past the censors: when Iris and Nick realize they only have 10 days for their love affair before they must escape Tokyo, Nick toasts: "Let's drink to them, the 10 days that shook the world." This juicy little morsel of Bolshevik propaganda is a direct reference to Sergei Eisenstein's cinema classic, as well as journalist John Reed's (the only Yank buried at the Kremlin, who was portrayed by Warren Beatty in 1981's *Reds*) account of the Russian Revolution. Both works were titled *10 Days That Shook the World* (the film is also known as *October*). Cole would pay for his insolence: not only was he blacklisted during the Cold War, but along with the rest of the Hollywood 10, he was imprisoned. He wrote his last movie, 1966's *Born Free,* under a pseudonym.

Although largely forgotten, the two-fisted *Blood on the Sun*, with its conspiracy theory about world domination that culminated with the Pearl Harbor sneak attack, is a trendsetter in the espionage and martial-arts genre. The battle between Cagney and Oshima, which involves martial arts, echoes in the clash between James Bond and Oddjob almost 20 years later in *Goldfinger*.

JUNGLE HEAT

United Artists, 1957

D: Howard Koch
S: Jameson Brewer
P: Aubrey Schenck
Cast: Lex Barker, Mari Blanchard, Glenn
        Langan, James Westerfield

Pre-Pearl Harbor fifth columnists create havoc in the industries and plantations of Hawai'i until an American doctor helps defeat them. Filmed on the island of Kaua'i in Hawai'i, the plot caused considerable controversy. No incident of sabotage or treason among Japanese or Hawai'i-born Japanese residents of Hawai'i could be confirmed during the war, except Ni'ihau.

CHAPTER 2
The December 7th
Attack on Hawai'i

THE DECEMBER 7TH ATTACK ON HAWAI'I

DECEMBER 7, 1941 is a defining moment for Americans of that generation as November 22, 1963, the assassination of President Kennedy, would be for Americans of a later one. Everyone remembers what they were doing, who they were with and where they were when they heard the dreadful news that forever would alter their lives. Wherever you were, on the farm or in the city, we were all connected by the radio and later the television to the events of those fateful days. The fact that the sneak attack and the huge loss of life happened on a Sunday, just several weeks before Christmas, added to the national sense of loss.

Perhaps succeeding generations mark their life calendars by the untimely death of rock stars like Elvis or John Lennon. Or might the events be the tearing down of the Berlin Wall, the Gulf War, the O.J. Simpson trial or the turn of the century? The immediacy and rapture of a nation gripped in a sense of loss by life-changing events has not happened in several generations.

Pearl Harbor thrust America into the modern world of electronic media. The nation's newspapers confirmed what we already knew: the U.S. would be at war with Japan and Germany. For many, this was a foregone conclusion by the time President Roosevelt's "Day of Infamy" speech to Congress was broadcast live on the radio across America and the world.

The average American did not have any idea where Pearl Harbor was, or even what it was, before December 7 etched it into the American psyche.

War movies have been popular with audiences since the beginning of Hollywood. *Birth of A Nation* (1915), *Hearts Of The World* (1918), *The Big Parade* (1925), *What Price Glory?* (1926), and *All Quiet on The Western Front* (1930) are just some of the better-known titles of the hundreds of films made. The

onscreen wars lent themselves to a parade of interesting characters, colorful costumes, flag-waving, sweeping action with hundreds of extras, explosions and stunts. Yet, the overwhelming majority of films produced during the war years were based in the Pacific theater of war.

During World War II Hollywood used combat action as an extension of the good guys-versus-the-bad guys formula. The German nazis and the Japanese soldiers were the clear-cut bad guys, as the communists would be just a few years later. One could say the modern-day action movie began with World War II.

Hollywood, with the cooperation of the U.S. Armed Forces, also produced films in order to boost recruitment and morale on the homefront as well as affirming the principles and values on which this country was based.

Initially, Hollywood quickly recognized that shame, embarrassment and loss were associated with Pearl Harbor and that public reaction to a title with such tragic overtones might result in poor box office, so they forfeited the use of Pearl Harbor in the titles of motion pictures. The American Film Institute catalog from 1940 to 1949 lists some 25 short and feature-length films that have Pearl Harbor as a subject, either as plot point, reference made or dialogue, but only one title using Pearl Harbor.

The first movies to represent America's involvement in World War II and Pearl Harbor-related themes all demonstrated American resiliency in the face of a disastrous event.

Remember Pearl Harbor was an excuse for a B-grade routine action movie about brave Yanks in the Philippines battling Japanese spies on the eve of December 7 and its aftermath. *Submarine Raider* demonstrated not only how unprepared we were to combat the Japanese in real life, but onscreen, as well. Until the Army and the government offered all the technical assistance necessary, it was difficult to make a modern war movie without access to guns, tanks, planes, ships and the like.

Air Force underlined the idea of Americans all having to work together to protect their country and its way of life through the symbolic use of the B-17 aircraft known as the *Mary-Ann*, in a feminine, Mother Earth womb-like context.

Viewed now, one can note that most of the films of the period did not show any American responsibility for the Pearl Harbor attack and blamed no one except the Japanese or Japanese fifth columnists working in the U.S. and its territories.

Air Force claims there were Japanese snipers on Maui and that Japanese vegetable trucks from Honolulu smashed into the planes at Hickam Field. Treachery is a key word, although no Japanese or Japanese-Americans were convicted of committing sabotage during the Pearl Harbor attack or during the war. It's no wonder that when John Ford made *December 7th* (in reality it was a re-creation, not a documentary), it was censored by the U.S. Navy because Ford criticized their lack of military preparedness.

Though there were rumblings and military advisors had warned of a Japanese attack in the Pacific, racism and cultural misunderstanding played into an underlying strategy that these "little yellow bucktoothed people" did not have the capacity or audacity to attack the U.S.

If an attack were to occur, the military theorized it would be in the Philippines or in Asia. As early as 1939, Congress (through the Hepburn Act) appropriated funds for the strategic overhaul and improvement of our overseas bases that included Pearl Harbor.

Most postwar films, such as *From Here To Eternity*, *In Harm's Way*, and *Tora! Tora! Tora!*, demonstrate communications mishaps, blunt errors and a relaxed attitude on the part of the military in Hawai'i before the attack.

Rather than relying on background shots, stock footage and studio interiors, advances in transportation brought about by wartime global mobility, and the development of lightweight camera equipment made it easier for postwar Hollywood to film Pearl Harbor stories in the actual locales.

From Here to Eternity, based on the realistic tone set by James Jones, was brought to the screen in a compelling version by screenwriter Daniel Taradash.

This was a more introspective and realistic view of life on an Army post in Hawai'i on the eve of Pearl Harbor. Whether Japanese planes actually bombed and strafed Schofield Barracks as the film depicts is immaterial. It became an exciting screen action forever etched in moviegoers' minds along with that famous love scene on the beach at Hālona Cove on O'ahu.

The Revolt of Mamie Stover, starring Jane Russell, recognized the role of the prostitute in the winning of the war, as did *From Here To Eternity*, but was diluted with production code restrictions and censorship that changed the world's oldest profession to the status of dance hostesses.

On the 20th anniversary of the attack, the Japanese Toho company produced *I Bombed Pearl Harbor*. This brought the war to American screens by the same people who also brought us *Godzilla*, and it showed, with miniature boats, planes and all.

By 1970, our former enemy's emerging economic strength and technological dominance was a recognized factor in the global marketplace.

Twentieth Century Fox's *Tora! Tora! Tora!* went all out to re-create Pearl Harbor by asking the Japanese to join in the production and tell their side of the story. It was mostly done with actual planes, ships and military facilities on Hawai'i and Japanese locations and is perhaps the most spectacular of the re-creations.

The films' textbook-like presentation, devoid of any real drama, left audiences cold, and *Tora!* was a box-office bomb. At the height of the politically charged Vietnam War era, Americans did not want to be reminded of a military defeat, no matter how glorious, and the youth audience did not seem to care.

Twenty years after the last major film on the subject and 60 years after the actual event, will advances in special effects and computer-generated imagery combined with a young cast and a love story make Michael Bay's $165 million *Pearl Harbor* a defining moviegoing experience for a new generation?

DECEMBER 7, 1941

aka December 7th—The Movie

U.S. Navy, 1943

**D: Lt. Commander John Ford, U.S.N.R.
and Lt. Gregg Toland**

P: U.S. Navy

C: Walter Huston, Dana Andrews,
Charley Grapewin

During World War II, Academy Award-winning director John Ford commanded the Allied Photography information effort for the Office of Strategic Services. Ford, a reservist, was chosen by Army general William "Wild Bill" Donovan, head of the OSS, to organize the film Photographic Unit.

John Ford's first film for the government was *Sex Hygiene* in 1941. This was followed by *The Battle of Midway* (1942), the first government documentary of the war years made expressly for viewing by the general public. Ford's next completed film was *December 7th*.

Ford's camera crew, headed by Gregg Toland, one of Hollywood's best-known cinematographers (*Citizen Kane*), arrived at Pearl Harbor six days after the attack that plunged the United States into war. Ford was reportedly incensed by the lack of preparedness and the ineptitude that had resulted in heavy losses. Ford's first 84-minute version of *December 7th* was a harsh indictment of the military, and, somewhat predictably, it was suppressed. It wasn't until 1943 that a 30-minute version which satisfied the Navy was released and won an Academy Award in 1943, though technically it isn't a documentary, since most of it has reconstructions or allegorical dramatizations.

The excised footage included a segment with Walter Huston as a complacent Uncle Sam vacationing in Hawai'i being warned by Charley Grapewin, as his conscience, about the loyalty of Japanese-Americans and about the military being unprepared. Of all the insipid personal stories in Pearl pictures, the meeting between Uncle Sam and Mr. "C" takes the cake. The other segment deleted was about the spirit of a dead Pearl Harbor sailor who reflects from the grave about America not being better prepared.

The original 84-minute version was restored and finally released by the U.S. Government in 1991 and was distributed on video for social and historical viewing purposes by Kit Parker Films.

Seen today, the restored film provides historical footage of prewar Hawai'i and its residents, but it is a racist and ignorant indictment—fueled by events and attitudes of the time—of Japanese-Americans and mixed-race residents of Hawai'i.

Footage from *December 7th* has been repeatedly borrowed by other documentary filmmakers as an authentic record of the attack on Pearl Harbor. It quite clearly is not, because, in truth, there were few cameras present during the event and John Ford was forced to re-create much of the action at Twentieth Century Fox Studio's backlot using miniatures with rear-screen or process photography. The carefully composed scenes of sailors running, falling and firing weapons were filmed later with actors. Thus the film represents one of the rare instances where moments of illusion have become, for most of us, the documentary reality.

One scene in *December 7th* shows soldiers attending a Sunday religious service. When the attack comes, they rush to their battle stations with the blessings of the priest.

AIR FORCE

Warner Bros, 1943

D: Howard Hawks

S: Dudley Nichols

P: Hal B. Wallis

Cast: George Tobias, Harry Carey, John
Garfield, Gig Young, Arthur Kennedy

Air Force begins on December 6, 1941, when the crew of the *Mary-Ann*, a B-17 flying fortress bomber, receives orders for a secret mission to Hawai'i and goes through various leave-takings at

Patterson Field near San Francisco. Flying to Hawai'i on a "routine mission," the radio picks up the shouts of Japanese fighter pilots. When the plane's radio brings in these first battle sounds of Pearl Harbor, one snoozing crew member comes to life and asks the radio man, "Hey Peterson, who've you tuned into, Orson Welles?" By the time they reach Pearl Harbor, the base is all flames and wreckage. The accompanying squadron seems to vanish. Alone, they first land on Maui and are attacked from the cane fields by snipers. After a stop at Pearl, the plane and its crew set out across the Pacific and encounter increasing problems. Finally, the condemned *Mary-Ann* is saved by a last-ditch effort by the survivors (with the help of the doomed soldiers in the Philippines). Damaged and out of fuel, the *Mary-Ann* finally crash-lands on an island beach near Australia after having spotted and reported a Japanese task force, and flying across the Pacific Ocean.

Air Force's plot was suggested by an actual flight of B-17s from the West Coast to O'ahu, which were indeed caught up in the Pearl Harbor events. However, fact and fiction soon part company. The film blames Japanese locals in Hawai'i who act as snipers and shoot at the *Mary-Ann* when the plane lands on Maui. At Hickam Field, Japanese "vegetable trucks" are blamed for acts of sabotage, including ramming a line of planes on the field. None of these acts ever happened and when the film was made they were known to be untrue. At the end of the film there is a small victory when the planes bomb a

Japanese task force as a symbol of American resiliency in the face of tragedy.

The film's location shots were done in Tampa, Florida, and Randolph Field in Texas. *Air Force* is the granddaddy of celluloid stereotypes regarding purported local Japanese fifth columnists.

REMEMBER PEARL HARBOR
Republic, 1942

D: Joseph Santley

S: Malcolm Stuart Boylan and Isabel Dawn

P: Albert J. Cohen

Cast: Donald M. Barry, Alan Curtis, Fay Mckenzie, Sig Ruman, Ian Keith, Rhys Williams, Maynard Holmes, Diana Del Rio, Robert Emmett Keane

Donald M. Barry (normally a Republic Pictures western star, usually billed as Don "Red" Barry) is the lead in this low-budget action movie that is the first film to show American troops in battle

[1.] John Garfield and Gig Young are aided by Marines in repairing their B-17 bomber at Clark Field in the Philippines in *Air Force*.

[2.] John Garfield, Harry Carey and Alan Jenkins watch the fire and wreckage of the aftermath of the Pearl Harbor attack from their B-17 as it heads for a landing at Hickam Field in *Air Force*.

Ground crew ward off an attack by Japanese Zeros on Clark Field in the Philippines in *Air Force*.

Luis Reyes Collection

SUBMARINE RAIDER
Columbia Pictures, 1942

D: Lew Landers

S: Aubrey Wisberg

P: Wallace MacDonald

Cast: Marguerite Chapman, John Howard, Bruce Bennett, Warren Ashe, Larry Parks, Forrest Tucker

The attack on Pearl Harbor was used to underpin this low-budget quickie yarn in which Sue Curry (Chapman) survives the shelling of her luxury yacht in Hawaiian waters by a Japanese aircraft carrier. She's picked up by a U.S. submarine that attempts to warn the American forces of the impending air strike on Pearl Harbor without success. The radio transmissions are jammed by the stronger radio frequency on the enemy carrier. The submarine captain's brother, Bill Warren, is a James Bond-like G-man who is fighting suspected spies and saboteurs in the Islands. He describes fifth columnists: "These nests have to be cleared out. They are poison to these islands and a lot more dangerous than we realize." Suji, his Japanese driver, aids in an attempt on his life. It is soon revealed that Suji has a hidden radio and tells an accomplice that it is time. The accomplice replies, "Everything is ready; fires will indicate position of most important naval units." (In real life, fires would have

action. Japanese envoy Kurusu's treachery is pointed out via newsreel clip, as are scenes of the havoc of the Pearl Harbor attack, to give a sense of realism to this fictitious story set in the Philippines.

American soldiers stationed at an Army post in the Philippines battle Japanese spies and discover the impending attack on Pearl Harbor and the invasion of the Philippines. The soldiers are sent on a patrol with a portable radio detector in search of a shortwave radio known to be broadcasting suspicious messages. Lucky Steve Smith (Barry) leaves his command to go back to town for a beer and a visit with his girlfriend.

The patrol runs into trouble without him. When they find the radio operator, a fight ensues and one soldier is killed as a result. Branded a deserter, Smith is arrested and escapes.

He finds a job working with the spy ring and sets out to right some wrongs, warning of the Japanese invasion of the Philippines on the same day of the Pearl Harbor attack.

In the end, Smith makes amends by crashing a bomber aircraft into a Japanese battleship and destroying himself together with the enemy. (This is similar to Kirk Douglas's sacrificial redemption in the 1965 film *In Harm's Way*, and the deadly real-life Japanese suicide kamikaze attacks.)

Republic was a low-budget studio with a strong reputation in the production of entertaining action, adventure and western stunt action films.

John Howard, Marguerite Chapman, Forrest Tucker and Bruce Bennett appear in one of the first films to utilize the attack on Pearl Harbor as the focus of the story in *Submarine Raider*.

Warren Ashe as a dinner-jacketed red-blooded James Bond-like U.S. government agent and his island-outfitted lady friend Eileen O'Hearn in a scene from the Columbia production *Submarine Raider*.

Opposite Page: Schofield Barracks under attack in 1953's Best Picture *From Here to Eternity*.

served no purpose with all of O'ahu completely visible in the morning light.)

The Pearl Harbor sneak attack is shown through the use of newsreel footage and through the running commentary of a morning radio host. The attack in the film begins at 7:30 A.M. instead of 7:50 A.M.

The film is full of stereotypes: yellow-menace spies, false walls and the like right out of a Saturday matinee serial. Again these early films blame treachery and fifth columnists, implicating Japanese-Americans in the attack.

In the end, the American submarine intercepts the aircraft carrier and torpedoes it, killing all on board. After lobbing shells to finish things off, Capt. Warren cries "Remember Pearl Harbor!" in retaliation for the attack and death of his brother.

All of these early war films mark the Pearl Harbor disaster measured against small victories due to the indomitable spirit and resourcefulness of the American fighting man.

FROM HERE TO ETERNITY

Columbia Pictures, 1953

D: Fred Zinnemann

S: Daniel Taradash, from the novel by
    James Jones...

P: Buddy Adler

Cast: Burt Lancaster, Montgomery Clift,
    Deborah Kerr, Frank Sinatra, Donna
    Reed, Ernest Borgnine, Philip Ober,
    Mickey Shaughnessy, Harry Bellaver,
    George Reeves, John Dennis

What is arguably the greatest of all Pearl pictures, ironically, did not take place at Pearl Harbor Naval Base, but rather at Schofield Barracks. It also did not have slam-bang special effects, and was shot in black and white. What *From Here to Eternity* did have was a superb, adult script by Daniel Taradash (who co-

wrote 1966's *Hawai'i*) that adapted the award-winning James Jones bestseller, as well as an unsurpassed cast, and superlative direction by Fred Zinnemann (fresh from 1952's *High Noon*). *Eternity* is the only Pearl picture, as well as the only shot-in-Hawai'i-feature, to win the Best Picture Oscar. Indeed, *Eternity* was showered with well-deserved nominations and eight statuettes, including the Academy Awards for the Best: Supporting Actor/Actress (Frank Sinatra, Donna Reed), Screenplay, Director, Cinematography, and others.

Eternity is a mature drama about Schofield Barracks officers, non-coms, and enlisted men (and their women) in the peacetime Army, set on O'ahu shortly before the Imperial air raid. Unlike many Hollywood movies, *Eternity* has a number of strong, well-drawn characters, and the subplots revolving around them are woven into a cohesive, comprehensive whole, producing a complex tapestry of emotion.

Perhaps *Eternity*'s most interesting character is Robert E. Lee Prewitt (the exquisite Montgomery Clift), the Southern rebel who tries to find a home in this man's Army. Prew is both a boxer and a bugler, suggesting the duality of man. He is also a hardhead, an individualistic square peg trying to fit into the prewar military's round hole—and he cannot. Captain Dana Holmes (Philip Ober) discovers Prew's pugilistic talent and becomes enraged when the stubborn Southerner refuses to put on the gloves again because he once blinded a man in the ring. Determined to win the regimental boxing championship, the career-climbing Captain orders Prewitt to undergo "the treatment"—running up and down Kolekole Pass with full field pack and rifle in the blazing tropical sun, and the like.

Cheating on his wife, Captain Holmes has transmitted V.D. to Karen (Kerr), rendering her unable to bear children. This in turn leads to her infidelity and reputation as a nymphomaniac. She has a torrid affair with her husband's right-hand man, Sergeant Milton Warden (Burt Lancaster), including their historic tryst on the beach at Hālona Cove as the waves surged about them. But Karen is no nympho—she's a passionate woman searching for true love.

1. Rare behind-the-scenes photo of Frank Sinatra as Maggio and Montgomery Clift as Prewitt before the cameras on location at Schofield Barracks, filming a sequence for *From Here to Eternity*.

2. Rare behind-the-scenes photo of Director Fred Zinnemann and crew giving last-minute advice to Deborah Kerr and Burt Lancaster, who prepare for the famous love scene at Hālona Cove on Oʻahu.

3

4

3. A "class" picture in every sense of the word. Sinatra, Lancaster and Clift pose with the men of the Hawai'i Infantry Training Center who worked as extras at Schofield Barracks for the filming of the Academy Award-winning film *From Here to Eternity*.

4. Frank Sinatra, Burt Lancaster, Deborah Kerr, novelist James Jones and director Fred Zinnemann leave Los Angeles airport for Honolulu location filming of *From Here to Eternity*.

The story also follows the love life of Prew, who falls for a prostitute named Alma (known professionally as Lorene). Sinatra plays Prew's pal and fellow dogface Private Angelo Maggio, a big-mouthed, brawling paisano full of bravado that lands him in the brig. There, the sadistic stockade sergeant, Fatso Judson (a chilling Ernest Borgnine before he chilled out in *McHale's Navy*), tortures Maggio. He escapes from the brig, but dies. Prew avenges his friend's death in an alley knife duel with Fatso, who manages to stab Prewitt before dying. Prew hides out at Lorene's Wilhelmina Rise home.

The Imperial air raid sweeps O'ahu. Sergeant Warden leaps into action. When an Army bureaucrat demands the proper forms before

In what may be the most famous love scene in movie history, Deborah Kerr and Burt Lancaster embrace at Hālona Cove, O'ahu, which locals nicknamed "From Here to Eternity Beach" after the movie based on James Jones' novel.

relinquishing arms—as Zeros strafe Schofield!—Warden and his men take forceful action against this symbol of military bureaucracy. Rushing to the rooftop with an automatic weapon, the heroic Warden downs a Zero.

When Prew finds out about the attack, against Lorene/Alma's wishes, the recuperating dogface insists on reporting for duty. He heads out to the frontlines in his aloha shirt, where soldiers are making fortifications in case of an enemy invasion. A hardhead to the end, the patriotic Prew fails to identify himself and is shot dead—by his own men.

The scene, shot at Wai'alae Golf Course, is a heartbreaker—one wants to shout out at the screen soldiers: "DON'T SHOOT! HE'S ON OUR SIDE!" James Jones' message is clear: the Army kills its best—and itself. During the McCarthy era, America ate its young, and could not tolerate nonconformity. The dissident individual must die. The film is a

reflection of McCarthyism and did boffo box office in the Soviet Union, while it was banned on some U.S. military bases, although James Jones' infantry unit today honors him at Schofield's post museum.

Clift's acting is transcendent (he, like *Eternity* co-star Lancaster, was nominated for Best Actor). In *Rebel Males, Clift, Brando, and Dean*, Graham McCann writes of Monty's method acting: "He demonstrates D.W. Griffith's boast that film 'photographs thought' when he faces the camera... In close-ups one is drawn to those eyes. Large, grey, infinitely expressive in his handsome but rather impassive face, they could register yearning, compassion, intelligence and despair in rapid succession. They articulate the ineffable, making Clift something of an auteur as he goes far beyond the screenplay. Indeed, the close-up of the eyes became a kind of signature."

After completion of the filming of interiors in Hollywood, the cast and crew of 100 flew via chartered plane to the Hawaiian Islands, where all the exteriors were photographed at essentially the identical locale of the novel. Approximately three weeks of shooting occurred at Schofield Barracks, the Royal Hawaiian Hotel, Waikīkī Beach, Diamond Head, the streets of Honolulu, and the Wai'alae Golf Course. It took three days to film the famous love scene on the beach between Burt Lancaster and Deborah Kerr.

One of the most exciting action sequences ever filmed by Hollywood cameras was the strafing of Schofield Barracks by Japanese Zeros. This re-creation of a phase of the attack on O'ahu, in which the Army installation was riddled by machine-gun fire as the Japanese pilots made their bombing runs on the Navy ships, was photographed at the locale of the disaster as described by novelist Jones.

(In fact, there is a dispute as to whether or not the Japanese actually bombed and strafed Schofield Barracks. What is now Wheeler Air Force Base, adjacent to Schofield, was a prime target because the Japanese wanted to knock out the U.S. planes there. Some contend that Schofield was hit by accidental fire aimed at Wheeler.)

A group of planes of the 199th squadron of the Hawai'i Air National Guard, bearing the familiar red "Meatball" insignia of the Japanese fighters, participated in the simulated attacks and the mock battle scenes featuring Burt Lancaster, the featured players, and the men of the Hawai'i Infantry Training Center.

The big screen version of this O'ahu-shot and -set drama is marred by its lack of local characters, who are only glimpsed in minor roles serving the white soldiers as bartenders, barmaids, and the like. As far as Native Hawaiians are concerned, the movie could have been called "From Here to Nonentity." The Imperial Japanese may have had Zeros, but to this film indigenous and local people were zeroes. After all, the Army really wasn't there to defend them anyway. (In the beginning of the novel, Prew has a brief affair with a North Shore AJA woman who, like her Japan-born parents, works on a plantation. Just as this was dropped for the film, Prewitt's homosexual activities were cut from the novel—there is a strange correlation here regarding the editing out of local characters, interracial love, and gay sex. But this book is already too long to go into that.)

The Thin Red Line is Jones' sequel (more or less) to *Eternity*, as his Infantry Battalion is shipped out to fight in the jungles of Guadalcanal. It's interesting to note that the first film version of *Red* was scripted by a blacklisted Red screenwriter, Bernard Gordon.

James Jones' daughter, Kaylie Jones, has emerged as a novelist and artist in her own "write." She wrote the autobiographical *A Soldier's Daughter Never Cries*, which the Merchant-Ivory team adapted into a fine 1998 film, with part-time Maui resident Kris Kristofferson portraying a fictionalized James Jones. Kaylie's fiction is poignant and powerful; 2000's *Celeste Ascending* is a contemporary story about a young woman who suffers from the premature death of her mother, and manages to emerge from an abusive romance. Kaylie is currently writing a World War II novel. She is closely involved with the James Jones Literary Society, which is dedicated to celebrating and perpetuating the legacy of that dogface who experienced it all at Schofield and Guadalcanal, wrote it all down, and found his place in eternity.

HELL'S HALF ACRE

Republic Pictures, 1954

D: John H. Auer

S: Steve Fisher

P: Herbert J. Yates

Cast: Wendell Corey, Evelyn Keyes, Elsa Lanchester, Marie Windsor, Nancy Gates, Jesse White, Keye Luke

In this low-budget crime melodrama, Chet Chester (Corey) is a restaurateur in Honolulu being blackmailed by an old buddy threatening to reveal

his past as a sailor in the Navy who was presumed killed during the Pearl Harbor attack. Chester's girlfriend (Gates) kills the blackmailer and Chester takes the blame for the shooting. A tip from a popular song written by Chester brings the three-day wife (Keyes) he left behind in the states when he shipped overseas with the Navy in 1941 to Hawai'i. She tracks him down and inadvertently gets involved in Chester's criminal activities.

The title *Hell's Half Acre* was taken from the former crime-filled skid-row section of Honolulu, which was razed in the late 1960s to make way for new buildings. The black-and-white film was shot partly on location in Honolulu, much of it at night. The song *Polynesian Rhapsody* by Jack Pittman is sung by the Kaumakapili Choir.

THE REVOLT OF MAMIE STOVER

Twentieth Century Fox, 1956

D: Raoul Walsh

S: Sidney Boehm, from the novel by William Bradford Huie

P: Buddy Adler

Cast: Jane Russell, Richard Egan, Agnes Moorehead

This is a story of an avaricious and ambitious woman who became the star of Hawai'i's best-known brothel. After organizing activities on an assembly-line basis, she made a fortune, invested it in real estate during the war and became one of the richest women in the Islands.

In San Francisco, Mamie (Russell) slides into a confidence game and is caught, but is permitted to board a freighter for Honolulu rather than go to jail. Aboard she meets Jim Blair (Egan), a Honolulu novelist who takes an interest in her. Mamie reports to her dance hall and finds it run strictly to make money by Mrs. Parchman (Moorehead) and her sadistic assistant, Adkins (Pate).

One of the rules of the establishment is that the girls will not have bank accounts

[1] Panic-stricken Honolulu residents run for the hills during the attack on Pearl Harbor in this scene from *The Revolt of Mamie Stover*. This photo was taken on location during filming. In the movie, special-effects matte shots are added at the studio to the background to simulate bombing, fires and smoke arising from Pearl Harbor that are not in this photo.

[2] Two famous figures—Jane Russell's and Diamond Head. Actress Jane Russell, actor Richard Egan and director Raoul Walsh on the beach at Waikīkī for *The Revolt of Mamie Stover*.

20th Century-Fox presents
The Revolt of
Mamie Stover
COLOR by DE LUXE
JANE RUSSELL · RICHARD EGAN
CinemaScopE
co-starring JOAN LESLIE

1

2

and ultimately Mamie asks Jim to handle her money. Jim takes on this responsibility; in time his emotions overpower his judgment and a real romance develops, to the dismay of his girl, the blue-blooded Annalee Johnson (Leslie).

Then comes the catastrophe at Pearl Harbor on December 7, 1941 and Mamie, unafraid, sees opportunity in the resultant panic. Because of the fear of an impending invasion, real estate prices drop, and Mamie, with cold hard cash in her hands, starts buying up prime properties. Jim enlists in the army and declares his love for Mamie. He tells her he will marry her at the end of the war if she promises to quit her profession. Mamie agrees but after his departure Mrs. Parchman offers her a bigger cut of her earnings at the dance hall. With Honolulu filling up with troops, it is a literal golden opportunity that Mamie cannot pass up.

Mamie becomes the darling of the Armed Forces and she wields considerable power and influence. Jim discovers through a promotional photo that Mamie has not left the profession and after being wounded he is sent home on leave. Mamie has believed that her tremendous material

success will vindicate her in Jim's eyes, but this is her moral failure. Jim disillusions Mamie when he tells her he can't marry her because he is no longer in love with her. Soon after we find the embittered Mamie, unbelievably, back in San Francisco at the dock where we first saw her, wearing the same clothes and carrying the same suitcase. The same cop is there to greet her. She tells him that she is on her way back home and that she gave away her fortune. This ending was tacked on by the censors and mars an already diluted story. (Another similar situation involving censors and prostitution occurs with the film *Miss Sadie Thompson* [1953] starring Rita Hayworth.)

Ninety percent of the exterior settings in *The Revolt of Mamie Stover* were shot on location in and around Honolulu. The cast and a crew of sixty people were flown to the Islands and remained there for a month of shooting. A variety of the world-famous beauty spots appear in the picture, including Waikīkī Beach, the terrace of the Halekulani Hotel, the Pali, Ala Moana Park, Punchbowl, the view from Kamehameha Heights and the Waiʻalae Country Club.

Hawaiʻi residents cooperated in full for the reenactment of the Pearl Harbor bombing. The Pearl Harbor sequence is five minutes long and comes in the middle of the film. This sequence is a mixture of location shots, special-effects matte shots and what seems like stock color footage from Ford's *December 7th*. The attack begins with Asian-American children outside the Chinese Christian Church trying to figure out what kinds of planes are flying overhead. A cop at a local diner having a cup of coffee hears some explosions and remarks that it must be target practice. Then over the radio comes the fateful news of an enemy attack. This is intercut with people literally running to the hills, planes overhead, bombs falling on ships, and sailors jumping from the bows of smoking ships into an oil-burning sea. Jim Blair at his hilltop home sees the bombs falling on Pearl Harbor; unable to communicate with Mamie via phone he makes his way through the crowded streets to her club. Bomb concussions rattle the nightclub as Mamie Stover and the girls run for the basement, but the astute Mamie realizes as she watches panicking civilians outside that this will be her last chance to cash in, when these same people will soon be evacuating.

Novelist William Bradford Huie (1910-1986) on whose novel this movie is based, was the author of hundreds of essays, articles, short stories, and

Luis Reyes Collection

21 books, including *The Americanization of Emily* and *The Execution of Private Slovik,* which were also turned into motion pictures.

I BOMBED PEARL HARBOR

Parade Releasing/Toho Company, 1961

Taiheiyo no Arashi [The Storm of the Pacific]

D: Shue Matsubayashi

S: Shinobu Hashimoto and Takeo Kunihiro

P: Toho Co., Ltd

Cast: Toshiro Mifune, Yosuke Natsuki, Makoto Sato, Misa Uehara, Tekashi Shimura

On December 8, 1941 (Tokyo time), the task force of the Japanese Imperial Navy successfully carries out the surprise attack on Pearl Harbor.

Koji Kitami, one of the many Japanese military men this event will significantly affect, is a sub-lieutenant assigned to an attack plane on the carrier *Hiryu.*

Koji, born in the country and raised by his widowed mother, graduated from the local middle school and then entered the Naval Academy at Etajima.

Upon his graduation he received his commission and expected a bright future.

After the long absence his schooling requires, he returns to his old home, basking in the love of his aged mother and the girl of his heart. Convinced that Japan will win the war he decides not to put off his marriage to Kiki.

On his wedding day, he receives two telegrams, one from his best friend and the other an order to return to his ship.

But Koji is sailing towards disaster. Unfortunately for Japan, all the code signals of the Imperial Navy have been decoded by the Americans, and the U.S. task force is waiting for the Japanese fleet at Midway. In one of the most decisive battles of World War II, the Japanese fleet meets a crushing defeat and Koji loses his best friend Matsuura as his ship goes down.

The Japanese military leaders are afraid the news of the defeat will become known to the people so the survivors of the fleet, including Koji, are confined to the Kanoya Naval Air Base in Kyushu.

And while Koji's young wife and mother are joyous over the false news of victory at Midway, he receives new orders to head south to an unknown destination on a journey of no return.

Jane Russell played Mamie Stover in this screen adaptation of William Bradford Huie's popular novel. Because of the film production code, Mamie's profession was changed from a prostitute to dance hostess.

[1] Imperial Navy pilots in the air on their approach to Pearl Harbor in the Toho company's *I Bombed Pearl Harbor*, produced by the same people who brought American audiences *Godzilla*, which certainly showed in the miniature work and special effects.

[2] Toshiro Mifune (center) as Admiral Yamamoto flanked by his officers in a scene from *I Bombed Pearl Harbor*. In reality Admiral Yamamoto was not on a carrier in Hawaiian waters during the attack, but led from his headquarters back in Japan.

This Japanese film was released in the United States in an English-dubbed version in time for the 20th anniversary of the Pearl Harbor attack in 1961. The title promises a lot more than it delivers as the Pearl Harbor attack makes up only the first twenty minutes of the color film. It offers little insight into the attack, which is re-created through the use of miniatures brought to you by the same company that produced the *Godzilla* movies. The flight miniatures and aircraft are passable, but when the planes reach Hawai'i, the simulated Hawai'i environments, including Kolekole Pass and the Ko'olau Mountains have no resemblance to the actual lush locations. The ships in the harbor look like toys. The film does manage to humanize the Japanese enemy somewhat through Koji, the lone pilot character we become familiar with, and the admiral played by Toshiro Mifune. It demonstrates the disillusionment of the young pilot who was told his country's forces were invincible when he faces the harsh realities of war at the crushing defeat at Midway.

Pilots take off from an aircraft carrier for the surprise attack on Pearl Harbor in *I Bombed Pearl Harbor*.

DeSoto Brown

Luis Reyes Collect. **RPH -**

IN HARM'S WAY

Paramount Pictures, 1965

D: Otto Preminger

S: Wendell Mayes, based on the novel by
James Bassett

P: Otto Preminger

Cast: John Wayne, Kirk Douglas, Patricia Neal,
Henry Fonda, Burgess Meredith, Tom
Tryon, Paula Prentiss, Jill Haworth, Dana
Andrews, Franchot Tone, Patrick O'Neal,
Carroll O'Connor, Larry Hagman, Hugh
O'Brian.

In Harm's Way is an epic black-and-white film that depicts the first years of the Pacific War.

In the opening scene, a carefree crowd watches aghast as Barbara Bouchet (Liz Eddington) practically pole-dances as she writhes sexily to the swing music solo at a conservative officers' dance on the night of Dec. 6. She leaves with airman Hugh O'Brien, and after an all-night tryst on the beach, they awaken to the roar of Japanese planes. Fleeing in O'Brien's convertible, the couple is killed when the car is forced off the road in an accident and explodes in flames as it crashes down a cliff. Meanwhile, the chaos of the Pearl Harbor attack is dramatically re-created in one of the few times that hints of the effects the disaster had on the civilian population.

The opening sequence (the attack on Pearl Harbor) was filmed "live" in the summer of 1964. One Hawai'i location in particular was literally set on fire. The ships of the United States Navy appear to have been bombed and strafed. But on film not one actual plane was used during the bombing sequence. The illusion of this infamous air attack was accomplished to a great extent by sound effects alone. As you view the film, you see two brief stock footage inserts of planes flying in formation, but you feel and hear the Japanese dive-bombers, the low-flying torpedo planes and the high-level fighters, as the Japanese air force, created by sound effects, cripples the United States Navy.

There are strong acting scenes and great overall production values since most of the film was shot on location in Hawai'i on military bases, utilizing Naval personnel and equipment. What mars the film is that most of the characters are very narcissistic and self-absorbed. There are motivating petty rivalries among those jockeying for positions of power among the Naval high command. There is very little feeling of patriotism or the world at large—a very narrow view, almost like a soap opera of the Big Brass. The result is that you don't much care about any of the characters or what happens to them. The finale is also marred by a battle sequence done with obvious miniatures—embarrassing even for the special-effects standards of the time.

The film contains a major sequence with para-Marines (airborne parachuting Marines) but there was no major parachute landing used in the Pacific Theater.

Kirk Douglas as Captain Eddington takes off from an airstrip in a PBY airplane on the right side, and any trained pilot would always commandeer an airplane from the left, where he would have easier access to the control instrument panels. A plane can be flown using the controls on the right side, but for a long flight this seems improbable. Nevertheless, his suicide mission to aid the success of Operation Skyhook is an act of redemption after he rapes a military nurse, who—he subsequently finds out—was engaged to the son (Brandon de Wilde) of Eddington's best friend, Rear Admiral Rock Torrey (John Wayne). Redemption is an underlying theme of this epic—de Wilde portrays Rock's estranged son, a poor little rich boy called Jer. However, inspired by his absentee Dad's heroism in combat, Jer quits a cushy bureaucratic job gained through political connections and goes into combat aboard a PT boat. This costs Jer his life, but he has

Spanish poster art work for the film *In Harms Way*. (Primera Victoria)

PEARL HARBOR IN THE MOVIES

Luis Reyes Collection

Luis Reyes Collection

[1.] A destroyer makes its way out of Pearl Harbor during the surprise attack in a scene from *In Harm's Way,* filmed on location in Pearl Harbor and other Hawai'i military installations. In reality a destroyer would have never attempted leaving the Harbor for fear of bottling up the entrance and exit to the Harbor in case the ship was hit and disabled.

[2.] John Wayne as Captain Torrey and Patricia Neal as nurse Lt. Maggie Haynes in a scene from *In Harm's Way*. Fifteen years previously the two stars worked together in similar roles in the Pearl Harbor-based *Operation Pacific*.

[3.] John Wayne as Admiral Rockwell Torrey, and Patricia Neal as Lt. Maggie Haynes in *In Harm's Way*.

[1] Kirk Douglas as Commander Paul Eddington and Jill Haworth as nurse Annalee Dorne, on location near Chinaman's Hat (glimpsed in the rear, on the right) at Kāne'ohe, on the windward side of O'ahu, just before the dramatic rape and murder scene in *In Harm's Way*.

[2] Burgess Meredith, Kirk Douglas, and John Wayne in Otto Preminger's sprawling WWII epic *In Harm's Way*.

been redeemed. History—in the form of the Great Crusade—gave people living petty lives the opportunity to ennoble themselves by fighting for a cause bigger than "me, myself, and I."

The Pacific islands referred to by the characters—such as Levu-Vana and Toko-Rota—are mostly made-up names, composites of actual oceanic isles. The former seems derived from Fiji, the latter from the Northern Marianas. Reprising their first affair in *Operation Pacific* (released 14 years earlier), the romance between Wayne and Patricia Neal (as a military nurse and daughter of an officer) is also noteworthy because of its warmth, tenderness, and maturity.

In a press conference scene held in a quonset hut during the island-hopping campaign, one war correspondent in particular asks Duke the most questions. The inquisitive newsman madly scribbles away in a reporter's notebook, and asks Rear Admiral Torrey (Wayne)—with the proper note of awe, admiration, and incredulity—"Are there any Japs left anywhere?" This brilliant piece of Method acting—or should we say typecasting?—is performed by movie star-cum-columnist Eddie Sherman, who first came to Hawai'i shortly after the Dec. 7 attack as part of the historic salvage operation which rescued so many of the damaged crafts. Sherman stayed on and went on, of course, to become one of Honolulu's best known journalists. (The other reporters in this scene were played by

actual local newsmen, and Honolulu impresario Tom Moffat, as well.) Carroll O'Connor and Larry Hagman also had small roles in the film, and went on to stardom as TV's Archie Bunker in *All in the Family* and J.R. Ewing in *Dallas*.

ADMIRAL YAMAMOTO

Toho Company, 1968

D: Seiji Maruyama

S: Seiji Maruyama, Katsuya Suzuki

P: Tomoyuki Tanaka

C: Toshiro Mifune, Toshio Kurosawa, Makato Sato, Koshiro Matsumoto

Toshiro Mifune, the quintessential samurai of Akira Kurosawa classics such as *Yojimbo* and *The Seven Samurai* (the source for *The Magnificent Seven*), stars in this biopic about the Commander-in-Chief of Japan's Combined Fleet. Despite Admiral Isoroku Yamamoto's misgivings over Tokyo's Tripartite Treaty commitments to the Axis powers, he devises the daringly desperate air offensive against O'ahu's military installations aimed at dealing a decisive blow, especially to the U.S. Pacific Fleet. The innovative strategy, which boldly included aerial torpedoing, was at that point the biggest carrier-launched aerial assault in history. After the Pearl strike is executed, the biopic follows Yamamoto to Imperial defeats at Midway and Guadalcanal. En route to the frontlines in Melanesia, U.S. warplanes acting on intelligence reports and high-level orders shoot down Yamamoto's plane, killing the Admiral.

In 1953, the Hollywood Reporter announced "Japs to Do War Pic," reporting that Toho Productions was inspired by the boffo box office of Hollywood's *Task Force* in Japan and would shoot a biopic about Yamamoto. It apparently took Toho 15 years to make the feature—perhaps wounds were too raw only eight years after VJ Day to make a picture about the man who bombed Pearl Harbor.

In 1968, the *Los Angeles Times*, however, was unimpressed by what Kevin Thomas called "this routine war picture with its vaguely semi-documentary tone." The veteran critic complained about Eiji Tsuburaya's special effects, "which all too obviously occur in the studio tank, which has been fitted out with a scale model of O'ahu and an array of miniature weaponry." Thomas groused about the talkiness of the biopic, much of which "takes place around conference tables, which scarcely makes for exciting entertainment… Unfortunately, it takes 45 of the movie's 130 minutes to get to the attack on Pearl Harbor…"

One of the oft-repeated cliches of Pearl pictures is the depiction of Yamamoto (who had lived in the USA) as a Shakespearian character, torn between his loyalty for emperor and country, and his awareness of the folly of rousing the sleeping Yankee giant. Thomas' main objection to this biopic is that it doesn't portray the Admiral's "private agonies of accepting a war he so vehemently opposed. The lack of this crucial scene is the movie's major weakness… Mifune… wast[es] his formidable talent and presence on mediocre ventures such as this… For those in the mood for Mifune 'Hell in the Pacific' [co-starring Lee Marvin and shot in Palau the same year] is by far the better bet."

TORA! TORA! TORA!

Twentieth Century Fox, 1970

D: Richard Fleischer

S: Larry Forrester

P: Elmo Williams

Cast: Martin Balsam, Sol Yamamura, Joseph Cotton, E.G. Marshall, Tatsuya Mihasi, Jason Robards, James Whitmore

This Japan-U.S. co-production is perhaps the most historically accurate big screen retelling of *Operation Hawai'i* in a feature. *Tora! Tora! Tora!* is unconcerned with typical titillating private lives saga: the only thing that matters in this script is reenacting the events leading up to the Battle of O'ahu and its execution. Shown are the Imperial strategizing and training; Japanese diplomats in Washington; U.S. intelligence scurrying about, trying to crack Tokyo's code; and an in-depth chronicling of the bombing and strafing of Pearl Harbor, Wheeler, et al, which is the meat of the film.

It's fascinating to see real-life Pearl characters brought alive and identified by name: Flight Commander Lt. Fuchida, who sent the "Tora! Tora! Tora!" ("Tiger! Tiger! Tiger!") signal that maximum surprise had been achieved; Admiral Yamamoto; Prince Fummaro Konoye, Japan's Prime Minister; General Hideki Tojo; strategist Commander Minoru Genda; Ambassador Saburo Kurusu; Secretary of State Cordell Hull; Secretary of War Henry Stimson; Lt. Commander Alvin D. Kramer of Naval Intelligence; Admiral Husband E. Kimmel; Dorie Miller; and those heroic lords of the air, Lieutenants Kenneth Taylor and George Welch (who apparently inspired the two lead characters in 2001's *Pearl Harbor*).

However, while *Tora!*'s no-nonsense, documentary-like retelling of the air offensive may be more factual and accurate than most Pearl pix, its lack of personal story and background makes for a rather cold, distant motion picture concerned more with history than with the individuals swept up in its world historical whirlwind.

The Hawai'i production of *Tora! Tora! Tora!* required logistics nearly as complicated as war. American airplanes of pre-World War II vintage were acquired from all over the world. Japanese planes had to be converted from other models. The company rented five old destroyers from the Navy, but hired the Maritime Services Division of the Dillingham Corporation in Honolulu to build a full-scale section of the USS *Arizona* at a cost of $1.5 million. Mounted on two steel barges, the 309-foot steel superstructure, fully fitted, was towed to Battleship Row to play her historic role.

Filming began on December 2,

Martin Balsam, as Admiral Kimmel in *Tora! Tora! Tora!*, watches the "Day of Infamy" unfold in a state of shock, as the American fleet is sunk at Pearl Harbor during the Japanese surprise attack. In this scene, a bullet whizzes through the window, narrowly missing the stunned admiral.

Opposite Page: Mounted on two steel barges, a full-scale section of the USS *Arizona* was built for the movie *Tora! Tora! Tora!* Her tower rose 144 feet into the air and was attacked, put under fire repeatedly, and finally destroyed four days before the end of filming in Hawai'i.

TORA! TORA! TORA!

For the first time once-warring nations combine to tell their true story of Pearl Harbour... History's greatest air-sea battle.

1

1. One of the few moments in the film where the effects of the attack on Pearl Harbor on the civilian population of Honolulu are shown in a scene from *Tora! Tora! Tora!*

2. The second assault on "battleship row" as filmed on location where it actually happened over the Ford Island Naval Base at Pearl Harbor, Hawai'i.

Opposite page. American soldiers take shots at approaching enemy planes in *Tora! Tora! Tora!*

2

1. *Tora! Tora! Tora!* press book.

2. The late Jason Robards, who stars as Lt. Gen. Walter C. Short in *Tora! Tora! Tora!*, was actually at Pearl Harbor on the day of the attack serving in the Navy aboard the USS *Honolulu*.

3. Mess attendant first class Doris "Dorie" Miller served aboard the battleship *West Virginia* and was the first African-American to receive the Navy Cross for Gallantry in World War II during the attack on Pearl Harbor. He is shown in the film *Tora! Tora! Tora!* (1970), though he is never identified in that movie or in John Ford's *December 7th* (1943). Finally in 2001's *Pearl Harbor* he is identified and played by Oscar-winning actor Cuba Gooding, Jr.

PRESSBOOK

The re-creation of the incredible attack on Pearl Harbor.

20th Century-Fox presents **TORA! TORA! TORA!** AN ELMO WILLIAMS-RICHARD FLEISCHER PRODUCTION

For the United States Sequences:
Starring MARTIN BALSAM as "Admiral Kimmel"
JOSEPH COTTEN as "Henry L. Stimson"
E. G. MARSHALL as "Lt. Col. Bratton"
JAMES WHITMORE as "Admiral William F. Halsey"
AND
JASON ROBARDS as "General Short"

For the Japanese Sequences:
Starring SOH YAMAMURA as "Admiral Yamamoto"
TATSUYA MIHASHI as "Cdr. Genda"
TAKAHIRO TAMURA as "Lt. Cdr. Fuchida"
EIJIRU TONO as "Adm. Naguma"
KOREYA SENDA as "Prince Konoye"
Directed by TOSHIO MASUDA and KINJI FUKASAKU
Assoc. Producer OTTO LANG

Screenplay by LARRY FORRESTER · HIDEO OGUNI · RYUZO KIKUSHIMA
Directed by RICHARD FLEISCHER   Produced by ELMO WILLIAMS   Music by JERRY GOLDSMITH
PANAVISION®   Color by DE LUXE®   [G] ALL AGES ADMITTED General Audiences

S I G

MAT—306

150 lines x 3 columns (450 lines)
3 columns x 11 inches

The Most Spectacular Film Ever Made!

DIRECT FROM ITS SENSATIONAL ROADSHOW ENGAGEMENT!
Now For The 1st Time At Popular Prices!

[G]   20th CENTURY-FOX

S I G

MAT—110

110 lines x 1 column (110 lines)
1 column x 7 7/8 inches

Luis Reyes Collection

2
3

Luis Reyes Collection

1968 aboard the aircraft carrier USS *Yorktown* portraying the Japanese carrier *Akagi*. On January 20, 1969, the planes came in low over the serene silent monument that covers the USS *Arizona* and dipped their wings in tribute to the men entombed there. This time, though, the planes were in the air to mark the opening photography of the film.

It was the start of three weeks of aerial and ground second unit photography headed by Ray Kellogg, Second Unit Director, whose film credits include *The Alamo* and *The Tall Men*. The aircraft tested in California were flown almost continuously from mid-December 1968 to late April 1969. Forty-seven experienced pilots, mostly on leave from the Air Force and Navy, comprised what came to be affectionately called the Fox Air Force.

Tora! Tora! Tora! was photographed at the actual locations in Hawai'i where it all took place: Ford Island, Hickam and Wheeler Fields, Kolekole Pass, Schofield Barracks, Waikīkī, Aloha Tower, the Kalihi district of Honolulu, Koko Head, Opana Point, Fort Shafter, and Chinaman's Hat.

In a historical slip, as the Japanese planes head over the hills toward Pearl, you can see the Schofield Cross in the background. The cross was actually built at Kolekole Pass to honor those who died in the attack years after it took place.

In the days before the attack, American planes at Wheeler Army Air Field, just across the road from Schofield, were moved into the open, where they could be guarded more easily. As the movie shows, the plan backfired. A few minutes into the attack on Pearl Harbor, Wheeler was hit by a formation of 25 Japanese dive-bombers, whose pilots must have been thrilled to see 140 fighter aircraft parked wingtip-to-wingtip. The Wheeler planes, vital to the defense of Pearl, were destroyed in minutes. It is widely believed that Lt. General Walter C. Short, commanding general of the Hawai'i department, shortsightedly ordered the planes out into the open and in these close formations to protect them from possible sabotage—in particular, from suspected AJA fifth columnists. Considering the fact that most AJAs remained loyal to America, it can be said that Uncle Sam paid dearly for Short's racist lack of faith with this sitting-duck tactic that cost O'ahu's defense and the war effort dearly.

Filming in Hawai'i went smoothly and on schedule, but in Japan problems occurred from the beginning. Akira Kurosawa, the most famous Japanese director of the time, was engaged to direct the Japanese sequences but was replaced by two

Japanese directors after he contractually failed to deliver the amount of footage requested. Two of Japan's most highly regarded screenwriters, longtime associates of Kurosawa, were enlisted to work on the screenplay. The Japanese sequences were filmed at Ashiya on the island of Kyushu; at Iwanai, on Hokkaido; and in Tokyo for exteriors of the Imperial Palace and the United States Embassy. Interiors were filmed at Toei-Kyoto and the Shochiku studios in Kyoto and also in Osaka.

Part of *Pearl Harbor* was shot at Kualoa Ranch, where many Hollywood movies—from *In Harm's Way* to *George of the Jungle* to John Wu's 2001's WWII action film *Windtalkers* starring Nicholas Cage—were, in part, also lensed. A movie museum in a WWII era tunnel at the Ranch documents films made at Kualoa, and tours there take visitors to see the footprints of Godzilla (who was created by nuclear testing in French Polynesia).

In a homage of sorts, the *Magnum P.I.* TV series featured an episode titled "Torah! Torah! Torah!", wherein a Torah is stolen from a Hawai'i rabbi. Tom Selleck investigates the theft of this scroll containing the first five books of the Old Testament that is used in a synagogue.

MIDWAY

Universal Pictures, 1976

D: Jack Smight

S: Donald S. Sanford

P: Walter Mirisch

Cast: Charlton Heston, Henry Fonda, James Coburn, Glenn Ford, Hal Holbrook, Toshiro Mifune

This star-studded, flag-waving film was promoted to coincide with the 200th anniversary of the founding of the U.S.A., and to stir patriotic feelings after the controversy of the Vietnam War with a film about America's last great justified triumphant war.

Filmed at Terminal Island Naval Base in Los

The famous admirals who were adversaries but never met in real life came face to face during the filming of *Midway* in the persons of two international film stars: Henry Fonda as Adm. Chester W. Nimitz, commander of the U.S. Pacific Fleet, and Toshiro Mifune as Adm. Isoroku Yamamoto, Commander of the Combined Japanese Imperial Fleet.

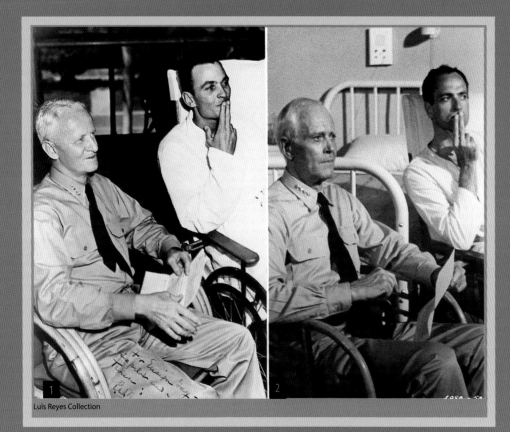

[1.] Photographed by Associated Press in 1942, Ensign Gay at a hospital in Pearl Harbor following the Battle of Midway, turning point for the U.S. in the Pacific in World War II. At this meeting, Admiral Nimitz was given a first eyewitness report of the battle by Ensign Gay, who after his bullet-ridden plane crashed into the sea, floated in the Pacific for 30 hours before rescue, and was a front-row witness to the epic battle that saw four Imperial aircraft carriers destroyed by U.S. Navy planes.

[2.] Newsworthy moment in history is re-created during filming of Universal's *Midway* by Henry Fonda, who portrays Adm. Nimitz, Commander of the U.S. Pacific Fleet, and Kevin Dobson, who plays the role of Ensign Gay, sole survivor of 30 officers and men of Torpedo Squadron 8, which attacked the Imperial Fleet.

[3.] Admiral Chester Nimitz (Henry Fonda), left, and his aide Lt. Commander Ernest Blake (Robert Wagner) are brought ashore in Pearl Harbor from a PBY flying boat following an inspection trip to Midway.

Luis Reyes Collection

1

2

3

Haruko Sakura (Christina Kokubo), an American of Japanese ancestry held in custody for internment during World War II, is comforted by Ens. Tom Garth (Edward Albert), who hopes to marry her.

Oppsite page Director Jack Smight (back to camera), rehearses *Midway* starring (from left) Henry Fonda, Robert Wagner, Charlton Heston, and Hal Holbrook.

[1.] In The Battle Plot Room at CINCPAC, Pearl Harbor, Planning the American defense of Midway in Universal's *Midway* are, from left, Chester W. Nimitz (Henry Fonda), Vice Adm. Raymond A. Spruance (Glenn Ford), and Vice Adm. William F. "Bull" Halsey (Robert Mitchum).

[2.] In the Battle Plot Room on the aircraft carrier *Akagi*, Vice Adm. Chuichi Nagamo (James Shigeta), center, discusses strategy with staff, Rear Adm. Kusat (Pat Morita), and Commander Genda (Robert Ito), right, prior to the Battle of Midway.

[3.] Katharine Ross, playing the secretary-aide of a United States senator, is menaced by an armed Japanese fighter pilot (Soon Teck-Oh) taken prisoner in *The Final Countdown*.

Angeles and in Pensacola, Florida, the film makes extensive use of stock WW II-era color footage shot by combat cameramen as well as certain cuts from *Tora! Tora! Tora!* (especially in the bombing of Midway Island scenes). There are many anachronisms in types of planes, naval equipment and ships that are shown. *Midway* has an interesting sub-plot involving a romance between a white U.S. military officer and a Japanese woman who's interned.

THE FINAL COUNTDOWN

United Artists, 1980

D: Don Taylor

S: David Ambrose, Gerry Davis, Thomas Hunter, Peter Powell

P: Peter Vincent Douglas

Cast: Kirk Douglas, James Farentino, Katharine Ross, Martin Sheen, Charles Durning, Soon Teck-Oh

The largest nuclear-powered aircraft carrier in the world, the USS *Nimitz*, encounters an unusual storm in Hawaiian waters that somehow transports the ship and crew back in time to the eve of December 7, 1941.

After the storm a series of events lead them to a nightmarish revelation. Their normal radio communications signals are not functioning, and they receive what they presume to be 1940s nostalgia broadcasting. They soon realize they've actually travelled back in time when a reconnaissance plane brings back aerial photos of Pearl Harbor with the USS *Arizona* and other 1941 vintage ships in the harbor.

A Senator Chapman (Durning) and his aide (Ross), while vacationing in a yacht off Hawai'i in 1941, are strafed by two Japanese fighter planes that destroy the yacht and kill the crew members before they can signal Honolulu. On a reconnaissance mission two jet fighters from the carrier spot the Japanese planes and are instructed to attack. The yacht survivors are rescued along with a Japanese pilot (Teck-Oh). Once on board, the survivors are amazed by all the modern machinery. The senator and his aide are isolated and the Japanese pilot is interrogated. During an onboard mishap, the pilot seizes a weapon and critically wounds two sailors, thus temporarily holding the ship hostage. When the executive officer reveals to him the Japanese attack plans are known, he is overcome and killed by Marines.

The modern-day characters believe they have a chance to change the course of history, preventing the Pearl Harbor tragedy by blasting the attacking air armada from the skies with the modern weaponry at their disposal. The captain believes that his duty is to protect the U.S. regardless if it is in the past, present or future.

While Senator Chapman and his aide are being transported to a small atoll with provisions for their own protection, the senator causes a deadly helicopter accident in which he and the flight crew are killed. The aide and executive officer are left behind on the atoll. The captain orders an attack on the oncoming Japanese planes and task force, the storm mysteriously reappears and envelops the ship and he aborts the mission. The USS *Nimitz* is again transported to the present.

Countdown was filmed in San Diego and at Norfolk Naval base, Virginia. Some stock shots

On December 7th, 1980 – The nuclear carrier USS Nimitz disappeared in the Pacific... and reappeared December 7th, 1941 ... off Pearl Harbor

Nothing in history could prepare you for

THE FINAL COUNTDOWN

KIRK DOUGLAS MARTIN SHEEN KATHARINE ROSS JAMES FARENTINO

Puzzled by a bizarre chain of events aboard the nuclear aircraft carrier USS *Nimitz*, civilian Warren Lasky (Martin Sheen), left, Commander Richard Owens (James Farentino), center, and Captain Matthew Yelland (Kirk Douglas) study their charts in *The Final Countdown*, a United Artists release.

1. Japanese planes strafe and explode a U.S. Senator's luxury craft in Hawaiian waters before it can radio back a warning to Pearl Harbor in *The Final Countdown*.

2. Kirk Douglas stars in *The Final Countdown* as Capt. Matt Yelland, commander of the USS *Nimitz*, the world's largest nuclear aircraft carrier, which is transported back in time to December 6, 1941 off the coast of Hawai'i. Peter Douglas (right) Kirk's son, produced the suspense thriller.

were interspersed at the beginning credits of Diamond Head and Pearl Harbor from the vantage point of an aerial helicopter transport.

The film has an interesting premise that the script does not fulfill. It plays like a big-budget episode of *The Twilight Zone* with very little dramatic impact. Unsatisfactorily, it settles for a sentimental ending involving a dog, a senator, a Naval officer who is left behind, and the girl he falls for. The star of this film is really the nuclear carrier USS *Nimitz*.

The film uses stock footage from *Tora! Tora! Tora!* and the classic newsreel footage of the *Arizona* burning with a voiceover by Roosevelt to convey the almost-averted Pearl Harbor tragedy.

A subdued Kirk Douglas as Captain Yelland, an awestruck Martin Sheen as civilian observer Lasky, and James Farentino as the ship's first officer Owens (and convenient resident World War II historian), carry the film forward and are provided excellent support by Charles Durning as the Senator and Katharine Ross as his ambitious and intelligent aide, Laurel Scott.

IMPERIAL NAVY

Toho Company, 1980

D: Shue Matsubayashi

S: Katsuya Suzaki

P: Tomoyuki Tanaka

C: Keiju Kobayashi, Toshiyuki Nagashima, Kanichi Kaneda, Yuko Kotegawa

Newsreel footage of the German invasion of Russia, the Imperial invasion of Indochina, and the halting of U.S. oil exports to Japan set the tone for *Imperial Navy*. A sort of Japanese *In Harm's Way*, this film has the epic sweep of WWII, following its Naval characters and their loved ones from Pearl to Midway to Guadalcanal to the Gulf of Leyte to Okinawa. This feature is fascinating because it depicts the Pacific campaign from a distinctly Japanese postwar point of view, referring to U.S. planes as "bandits"—an insult that would warm the heart of any censor of Hollywood's wartime propaganda.

Masato is accepted as a Navy cadet, and outranks his veteran father when he's drafted. After the tide of war turns against Japan, Masato is on leave in his rural, traditional village, where lovely scenery and a pagoda are glimpsed. In the aftermath of the defeats at Midway and Guadalcanal, Masato's

fearful he won't survive the war, and asks his betrothed to call off their engagement. Yoko replies: "What was the first thought that went through your mind when you saw me? Was it 'Tora! Tora!'?" Masato must suddenly return to his base, and in departing the cadet salutes his father.

In 1944, mechanics aboard a carrier are distraught about the suicide missions of the young kamikaze. Before takeoff, the chief orders the pilots to "stay alive," and gives the lucky charm he's carried since Pearl to a young flyboy. Masato, who's become a pilot, is in his cockpit, and he imagines Yoko. Meanwhile a kamikaze is shown as it bursts into a carrier. Admiral Halsey (unseen) falls for a diversion (although James Cagney doesn't in his Halsey biopic "The Gallant Hours"), and the Japanese argue among themselves over tactics during the Leyte Gulf battle.

Back at the homefront, the press wants to interview Masato's mother, who believes she's lost both of her boys and weeps at a shrine with candles and photos of her sons. When Masato's younger brother Ensign Hanjo shows up, his father is overjoyed, but Hanjo is rueful. Masato had given his kid brother a life jacket, and the ensign says: "I know he died so I could live." Yoko is present during this poignant scene.

In a farewell letter to his brother, Masato expresses his last request: "Yoko's a wonderful girl. Look after her, marry her." (In *Pearl Harbor*, before Rafe goes off to the Battle of Britain, he tells his friend Danny to take care of his girlfriend Evelyn if anything happens to him.) But when he's abruptly assigned to the Yamato battleship, Hanjo tells Yoko she should forget about him. "What do you think I am? A doll that men can pick up and put down at will?" Yoko retorts. Hanjo agrees to marry her that day.

During Hanjo's leave, his veteran father asks his son if he's a kamikaze and disagrees with the suicide missions, saying the flyers "die for nothing… die in vain." The parent seems to change his mind when told it's a high-command order.

Back aboard ship, an admiral writes what he thinks is his last letter to his two daughters. The canteen is opened, a Shinto priest brings drinks, which are offered free to the pilots. The flyers banter—"Ready to die?" "Sure, anytime," one replies. They sing drunken patriotic songs. In the bunks, a serviceman cries. Ensign Hanjo looks at Yoko's photo, and thinks of his wife.

During the April 1945 battle of Okinawa, Hanjo's father watches his son—who salutes him—

take off from the carrier deck. There's an action-packed engagement apparently incorporating actual color documentary footage. Yoko's husband is pinned down. The kamikaze pilot's father valiantly tries to put out a shipboard fire; although the water valve is blazing hot, he heroically turns the valve and releases the water, severely burning his hands. The Vice Admiral sees the ship's afire, and dead sailors are in water on the ship. High above, Hanjo watches the carrier explode. He salutes and says: "Father, I didn't die before. But now it's my time to go… Sayonara."

Imperial Navy ends on a slightly hopeful note. Yoko is on a beach with her little son, who frolics in the water as Suinji Tanimura's plaintive song "Gunjo" is heard. As in Kurosawa's 1970 "Dodes'ka-den," Japan will survive its long national nightmare, and future generations will have a brighter future…

Imperial Navy begins with high-ranking Naval officers planning the Pearl attack, greatly compressing the time from the conception, strategizing, and preparing for the carefully laid-out aerial sortie to its December 7, 1941 execution. According to Gordon W. Prange's definitive *At Dawn We Slept: The Untold Story of Pearl Harbor*, Yamamoto, the Commander of the Japanese fleet, actually said to Vice Admiral Shigeru Fukudome: "I wonder if an aerial attack can't be made on Pearl Harbor?" in the first half of 1940. In "Imperial Navy," an admiral asks "Why don't we send our planes to Hawai'i?", and the deployment takes place shortly afterwards.

The Pearl Harbor special effects directed by Teruyoshi Nakano—brought to you by Toho, the same folks who gave us *Godzilla*—are cheap, cheesy, unrealistic, and apparently use the same footage as *I Bombed Pearl Harbor*. The studio-shot model ships, mock-up of Kolekole Pass, etc., pale in comparison with the far more sophisticated *Tora! Tora! Tora!*—let alone the high-tech CGI effects and cinematography, etc., of 2001's *Pearl Harbor*. From a technical perspective, *Imperial* and *I Bombed* are to Pearl pics what the actual attack was to the U.S. Navy. (They're badly dubbed in English, to boot.)

This sub-genre's much-filmed scene, which could be dubbed "admiral agonistes," follows the attack: in the war room, the commander asks, "Can you tell me why there were no carriers…they weren't there today. Our victory is meaningless." In *Imperial Navy*, this is followed by the narrator's suggestion that Pearl was a sitting duck due to an FDR scheme to end American isolationism and enter the war.

In the feature, Yamamoto's fateful flight to Bougainville is shot down on the correct date—April 16, 1943. "I always knew that war was hell," the Shermanesque, bleeding Admiral says shortly before dying.

Imperial Navy's antiwar theme reflects Japan's postwar framed rules (the world's first anti-nuclear constitution) which forbid war. Told from a Japanese perspective, war is seen as a doomed, futile endeavor—unlike in most American Pearl pix, where inevitable victory is a certainty. But for Western audiences used to samurai stereotypes, the film's grieving parents and girl-back-home romance may come as a revelation. We have met the enemy, and while he may not exactly be us, he's neither subhuman or extra-human, but rather quite human after all, with our same foibles, frailties, heroism, and dreams. To the extent that *Imperial Navy*'s homefront story in particular humanizes the Japanese, it is a worthwhile, if flawed, endeavor.

PEARL HARBOR

Buena Vista, 2001

D: Michael Bay

S: Randall Wallace

P: Jerry Bruckheimer

Cast: Ben Affleck, Cuba Gooding Jr., Jon Voight, Josh Hartnett, Kate Beckinsale, Carey Hiroyuki Tagawa, Alec Baldwin, Dan Aykroyd, Mako

NOTE: Like all references to this feature in this book, the following is based on preliminary information.

In 1926 Tennessee, Rafe McCawley (Ben Affleck) and Danny Walker (Josh Hartnett) are boyhood pals who grow up with a love of flying derived from Rafe's father, a World War I flyer turned crop duster. In turn Rafe tries to protect Danny from the wrath of his crippled father, who's also a veteran. Following a quick montage of newsreel images of Nazi and Imperial aggression, by January 1941 the childhood chums are in their early twenties, and have enlisted as Army pilots. Flying P-40s, they train at a New Jersey airfield under base Commander Jimmy Doolittle (Alec Baldwin).

Rafe falls in love with Lt. Evelyn Stewart, a military nurse whom she meets when she injects his okole with a hypodermic needle and allows the somewhat dyslexic Rafe to pass the eye exam, enabling him to continue his career as a pilot.

Colonel Doolittle informs the top-gun-like Lt. Rafe McCawley that his application to serve in the American Eagle Squadron (U.S. flyers supporting Britain against German air raids before Washington officially entered WWII) has been approved. However, he has not informed his best friend or sweetheart. The night before his departure to the front, the conflicted Rafe tells Evelyn, and does not make love with her.

Rafe is shipped out to England, and he and Evelyn continue to correspond and profess their deep love for one another. Rafe is shot down in a dogfight during the Battle of Britain and reported dead.

Evelyn and Danny have been transferred to Pearl Harbor. They both grieve for Rafe, who had told Danny to take care of Evelyn if anything happened to him. Eventually, Danny and Evelyn become lovers.

In early December 1941, Rafe—who has miraculously survived being shot down—pops up at Pearl Harbor. He quickly figures out what's been going on while he was presumed dead, and fights with Danny in a barroom brawl and beyond. Meanwhile, the Imperial task force carrying Admiral Yamamoto and his Zeros bears down on Hawai'i, as U.S. military intelligence in Washington and Pearl increasingly suspect Tokyo is up to some deviltry.

Rafe and Danny awake on December 7, 1941, as Imperial Japan strikes. Taken by surprise from Ford Island to Battleship Row to West Loch to Wheeler to Hickam, the U.S. forces are decimated in graphic, living color. The USS *Arizona* is blown to smithereens, and the USS *Oklahoma* rolls over. USS *West Virginia* boxing champ and mess attendant Dorie Miller mans an anti-aircraft gun and shoots down a Zero.

Putting aside their petty squabble, Rafe and Danny manage to get two P-40s in the air and engage the enemy. An exciting dogfight takes place low over Ford Island, with aircraft zooming low past buildings, and Rafe and Danny performing barnstorming tricks they'd learned back in small-kid days. (This may be one of the most sit-on-the-edge-of-your-seat chase scenes since Steve McQueen in 1963's *The Great Escape* and 1968's *Bullitt*.) As O'ahu is bombed and strafed, Evelyn steadfastly takes command in the hospital, as she rallies the nurses, aids the wounded, and is put in charge of triage.

On the bridge of an Imperial flattop, Commander Genda recommends launching a third wave. But Admiral Yamamoto decides against it, and the task force turns back. Evelyn continues her work at the hospital. Amidst the smoke-filled carnage of Battleship Row, Admiral Kimmel receives a telegram telling him to be on alert for a possible Japanese attack—delivered too late to be of use.

Rafe and Danny join rescue workers who save swabbies trapped inside the capsized USS *Oklahoma*. On the bridge of his carrier, amidst the irrational exuberance of his men, Admiral Yamamoto is reflective, and expresses his fear that all the sneak attack has done is "awaken a sleeping giant, and fill him with a terrible resolve." President Roosevelt (Jon Voight), metal leg braces and all, delivers his "date which shall live in infamy" declaration of war to Congress, America, and the world.

In a White House meeting with General George C. Marshall, FDR resolves to expeditiously strike back at Tokyo. When told such a mission is impossible, the Chief Executive manages to rise from his wheelchair to make a point. Rafe and Danny—who are now war heroes and just about the only U.S. pilots with combat experience—are recruited for the top secret mission. Evelyn visits Rafe alone in his hotel room as he packs, and tells her ex-boyfriend that she'll never leave Danny because she's pregnant now. Evelyn makes Rafe swear he won't tell Danny before their mission is accomplished.

Danny and Rafe train with Colonel Doolittle. In April 1942, they fly two of the 16 B-25 bombers launched from the deck of the USS *Hornet*, and bomb Tokyo. In a Naval intelligence

The clouds of black smoke re-created here for the *Pearl Harbor* location shooting make it similar to documentary footage of the devastation wrought on "Battleship Row" on December 7, 1941.

Members of the *Pearl Harbor* cast, a National Park Ranger, and a Pearl Harbor survivor pay homage at the wall bearing the engraved names of the victims of the bombing and sinking of the historic battleship at the USS *Arizona* Memorial.

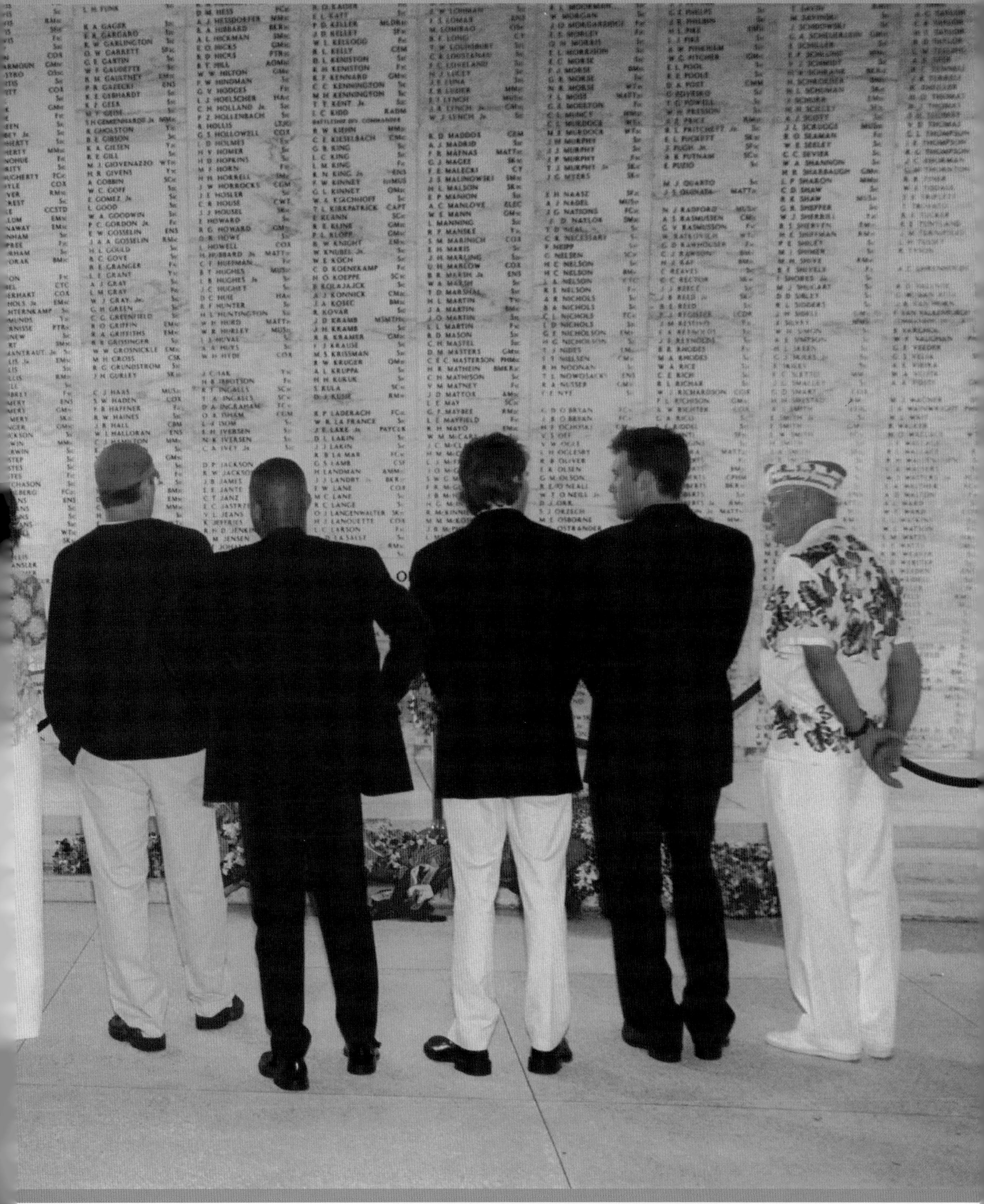

A JERRY BRUCKHEIMER PRODUCTION

PEARL HARBOR

A MICHAEL BAY FILM

Movies are often shot in Hawai'i, and location lensing requires public awareness and cooperation—especially when re-creating the most infamous military defeat in American history. Here, a crew sign warns Islanders about the reenactment of the December 7th, 1941 aerial assault on O'ahu for the Pearl Harbor feature.

monitoring room at Pearl, Evelyn manages to listen in on the incursion as it's in progress. Doolittle's Raid proves that Japan is not invulnerable, and raises American morale—but at a terrible price. In emergency and crash landings, Rafe and Danny make it to the coast of China. As a Japanese patrol closes in on Rafe's crew, Danny soars out of the sky, and his turret gunner mows the enemy down, before he crashes. Danny is injured in the crash, and he and Rafe are captured by Imperial soldiers. A shoot-out ensues, and Chinese allies arrive and save the U.S. flyers.

However, a soldier has shot the already wounded Danny in the stomach. Rafe tells Danny not to die, revealing he's about to be a father. "No. You are," Danny replies, dying. As the Doolittle heroes return to Pearl, Evelyn's voice is heard: "It was a war that changed America…World War II began at Pearl Harbor, and 1,177 men still lie entombed in the *Arizona*. America suffered. But America grew stronger. It was not inevitable. The times tried our souls, and through the trial, we overcame." In the White House, FDR hands Doolittle a Medal of Honor, and gives two to Rafe.

Evelyn and Rafe, who holds a baby boy, are at a memorial to Danny at a Tennessee crop-dusting landing strip. Rafe calls the child, who wears one of the Medals of Honor, Danny, and asks the lad if he wants to fly.

Pearl Harbor reunites the Jerry Bruckheimer/Michael Bay/Touchstone Pictures team and repackages the formula of an action-packed macho movie full of expensive, explosives-laden special effects, aimed at the *Lord of the Flies* teenage male

demographic that drives the Hollywood box office. Producer Bruckheimer, director Bay, and Touchstone are the fine folks who gave us the mostly mindless action films *Bad Boys* (1995), *The Rock* (1996), *Gone in 60 Seconds* (2000), and, along with *Pearl Harbor*'s leading man Ben Affleck, 1998's *Armageddon* (which *P.H.* screenwriter Randall Wallace also wrote). With its reported 180 digital effects and juvenile romance, as well as frequent puerile scatological references, *Pearl Harbor* promises to be more of the same.

The reportedly $165 million Disney epic seems aimed at the same teen market which made 1997's *Titanic* such a worldwide box-office hit. *Pearl Harbor* has similar elements—young romance, a love triangle, watery disaster, and an ingenue named Kate (Beckinsale, not Winslet)—except, as screenwriter Randall Wallace points out, the *Titanic* took six hours to sink, while the *Oklahoma* took only six minutes to go down. Similarly, *Armageddon*'s asteroid on a collision course with Earth has become the Pearl Harbor Strike Force.

Pearl Harbor reprises many of the tried and true staples of Pearl pictures. There is the soap opera-ish personal story, sexual dysfunction, and disloyalty. The infidelity unleashes the infidels—and, in the end, Danny must pay for his disloyalty, big time. It is interesting to note that African-American Navy steward Dorrie Miller—a character that also appears in both *Tora! Tora! Tora!* and Ford's *December 7th* manning a machine gun to defend himself against the air attack—is identified by name for the first time in *Pearl Harbor* (played by Academy Award-winning actor Cuba Gooding, Jr.). To the film's credit, Miller was indeed the USS *West Virginia*'s heavyweight boxing champion and mess attendant, although the type of weapon he actually fired is disputed.

Far more grave is the misrepresentation of Admiral Yamamoto, who is depicted as being on the bridge of the carrier *Akagi* in the Imperial task force that carried Operation Hawai'i. The fact is, Isoruku Yamamoto was nowhere near the *Akagi* or any of the other ships that launched the O'ahu offensive—he was thousands of miles away at Kure Naval Station, Japan, aboard his flagship, *Nagato*.

As depicted in *Pearl Harbor*, following the foray, Yamamoto did have regrets (albeit in Japan, not on board the *Akagi*). But as in *Pearl*, this film does not reveal what Yamamoto is most concerned about: the fact that the U.S. carriers were not in port, and therefore escaped destruction. *Pearl Harbor* recruited a crew of 500, plus 1,000 extras, many from Hawai'i. Yet, in the legacy of most Pearl pics, it almost completely ignores the local population. AJA Little Leaguers are briefly glimpsed eyeballing the Imperial aircraft soaring low overhead. There's also an AJA listener at an O'ahu surveillance base spying on a phone call to Japan, and the AJA character in the mission monitoring room where Evelyn overhears news of the Doolittle Raid does have a few lines of dialogue. The bouncer at the surf bar where Rafe and Danny beef is—you guessed it!—a Samoan.

But there is not a single solitary significant Hawaiian or other local character in the entire movie, leaving Islanders voiceless and transparent in their own land. Twenty-plus years after *Pearl*, there is no Holly Nagata. What about the estimated 68 dead and 35 wounded locals? Do they matter?

Nonetheless, in addition to rock-'em-sock-'em state of the art digital special effects, *Pearl Harbor* does have some originality. The use of child abuse as a metaphor for the Imperial bully is clever.

Depiction of a Navy newsreel cameraman is refreshing. The rescue of trapped seamen in the *Oklahoma* is a laudable addition—the aftermath at Pearl, in terms of these rescue missions (and the ensuing salvage operation), is rarely dealt with in Tinseltown features. Inclusion of the Doolittle Raid is brief but also noteworthy.

However, when all is said and done, if *Pearl Harbor* succeeds in rekindling interest in this defining moment in American and world history (especially among an ahistorical generation) many of whom may have never even heard of Pearl Harbor, the screen epic's virtues shall greatly outnumber its vices.

As Governor Cayetano told the *Star-Bulletin*: "There are too many generations of Americans who don't know the Pearl Harbor story. This movie will help this generation and generations to come" to learn about and relive the days of infamy and glory.

Zeros attack a U.S. warship in the special effects-filled *Pearl Harbor*, which reportedly uses up to 180 digital images.

Dennis Oda

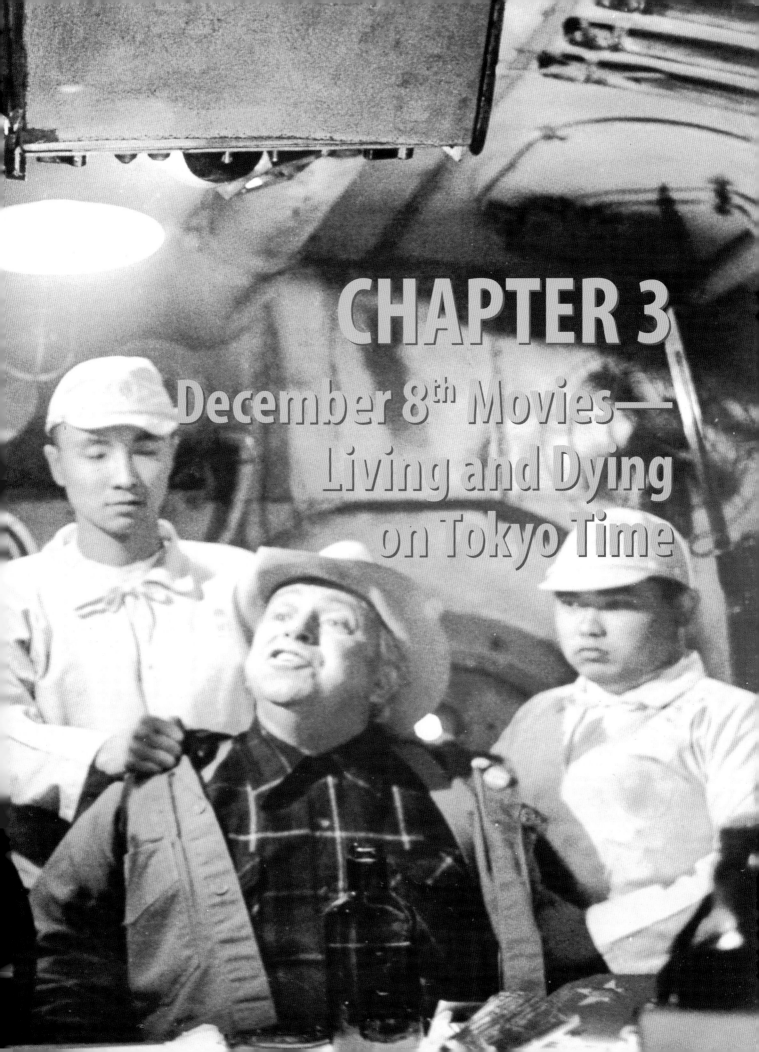

CHAPTER 3
December 8th Movies—
Living and Dying
on Tokyo Time

DECEMBER 8TH MOVIES
LIVING AND DYING ON TOKYO TIME

THE WORDS "PEARL Harbor" conjure up a specific Naval base and air attack—up until that time, the largest carrier-launched strike ever. The Japanese midget (and other) subs that invaded Hawaiian waters are generally overlooked in films about December 7, 1941. Even more significant is the fact that the aerial assault affected far more than just the Pearl Harbor geographic area itself. You didn't have to look down from Makalapa Heights or be on Ford Island to see combat. Military facilities at Hickam Field, Schofield Barracks, Wheeler Field, Kāneʻohe Naval Air Station, Bellows Field, etc., were all bombed and/or strafed. Even if the Leeward Naval installation may have been hardest hit and the focus of the blitz, rather than the appellation of "Pearl Harbor," "The Battle of Oʻahu" would be a more accurate name for what happened. Indeed, with the B-17s en route from California making emergency landings on the Neighbor Isles, and an Imperial pilot making what may be the only 20th-century trip to Niʻihau not authorized by the Robinson family, the most appropriate term for what happened might be "Operation Hawaiʻi" (as Japanese strategists called Admiral Yamamoto's plan).

Furthermore, not only is the perception of events that took place on December 7 Pearl Harbor-centric, it is, for Americans, very much centered on the U.S.-ruled Territory of Hawaiʻi. But, in addition to the T. of H., other U.S. possessions and territories came under attack that day. Furthermore, so did a number of other Asian colonies and countries. Indeed, what Americans commonly refer to as Pearl Harbor is really the tip of the iceberg. Stretching across the International Date Line, the Imperial operations of December 7/8, 1941, from the tip of the Polynesian triangle to the Asian continent, may be the largest, most far-flung, coordinated military offensive in the history of warfare. Attila the Hun, Genghis Khan, Julius Caesar, Hannibal, Charlemagne, Napoleon, Mussolini, and even Hitler never launched an offense of such breadth and scope in a single day. The world has never seen anything like it—before or since.

When Flight Commander Mitsuo Fuchida flew past Barbers Point at 7:53 a.m. and signaled the Imperial Navy that maximum tactical surprise had been attained with the code words "Tora! Tora! Tora!" ("Tiger! Tiger! Tiger!"), far more than Pearl Harbor was attacked by surprise. According to John Costello's *The Pacific War 1941-1945*, at 5:45 a.m. (all of the following times are Hawaiʻi time, December 7, 1941), the forces of General Yamashita—the "Tiger of Malaya"—began invasion of Kota Bharu, in the British colony of Malaya (now Malaysia). At 6:12 a.m., Japanese planes bombed a U.S. seaplane tender in the Gulf of Davao, Philippines. Yamashita's forces landed at Kra Peninsula, Thailand, at 7:30 a.m. By 10:00 a.m., the Battle of Oʻahu was over, but in Shanghai, China, Lt. Commander Columbus D. Smith was arrested by Japanese guards as he tried to board his ship. A British gunboat was sunk by Imperial artillery. An Imperial air raid bombed Singapore at 11:30 a.m. Japanese Naval bombers attacked the U.S. territory of Guam at 12:57 p.m. Three minutes later, another U.S. possession, Wake Island, was bombed and strafed. Thirty-five dive bombers attacked the British colony of Hong Kong at 2:00 p.m., and Japanese infantry battalions started moving in from China. Northern Luzon, Philippines, was bombed at 3:00 p.m. Aerial bombardment of Clark Airfield at 5:30 p.m. knocked out much of U.S. air power in the Philippines. At 12:31 a.m., December 8, Hawaiʻi time, Japanese destroyers shelled Midway.

What a difference a day makes! By May 1942, the flag with the rising sun insignia fluttered over all of the above (and more)—except for Hawai'i and Midway, where, hard on the heels of the May 8 Allied victory in the Battle of the Coral Sea, the war slowly, inexorably started to turn around. In this section, we take a look at feature films depicting the Imperial offensive of December 8, 1941, on the other side of the International Date Line, as well as some movies with scenes set on the homefront on or about the day of infamy.

WAKE ISLAND

Paramount, 1942

D: John Farrow

S: W.R. Burnett and Frank Butler

P: Joseph Sistrom

Cast: Brian Donlevy, MacDonald Carey, Robert Preston, William Bendix

The first attack on Wake Island came on December 8. After that, raids came daily. On this flat, sand-covered coral reef, which had no shelter from the air, Japanese planes rained destruction for 16 days. The island was held by 385 U.S. Marines and some civilian workmen. This was a tiny force, but so dauntless that after ten days of bombardment, they defiantly radioed: "Send us more Japs."

The film was shot on location in the sand dunes at Salton Sea in the California desert. The real war caused unusual problems for the filming company. All the Japanese extras had been interned by Executive Order 9066, so Hollywood had to train Filipinos and Mexicans to play the part of the Japanese enemy. In order to fly planes bearing the rising sun on their wings over the movie's locale, Paramount (with permission from the Army authorities) had to warn all the antiaircraft stations and nearby inhabitants in the area that its Japanese planes were

Luis Reyes Collection

in actuality American aircraft with enemy insignia for the filming of the movie. *Wake Island* was nominated for four Oscars.

DeSoto Brown Collection

[1] MacDonald Carey, Robert Preston and Brian Donlevy are among a handful of Marines who must face the onrushing Imperial fleet in this powerful true-life World War II drama , *Wake Island.*

[2] Robert Preston and William Bendix relax between takes with a canine pal at the Salton Sea , California, location doubling for *Wake Island.*

MANILA CALLING

Twentieth Century Fox, 1942

D: Herbert I. Leeds

S: John Larkin

P: Sol M. Wurtzel

Cast: Lloyd Nolan, Carole Landis, Cornel Wilde

Lloyd Nolan stars as the leader of a band of Americans who form a guerilla unit and fight on after the Japanese invasion of Mindanao until the enemy closes in and wipes them out.

THE FLYING TIGERS

Republic, 1942

D: David Miller

S: Kenneth Gamet and Barry Trivers

P: Edmund Grainger

Cast: John Wayne, John Carroll, Anna Lee, Paul Kelly, Gordon Jones.

The American Volunteer Group or Flying Tigers fight bravely for China's freedom despite being greatly outnumbered. Squadron Leader Jim Gordon (Wayne) gets a new recruit when Woody Jason (Carroll) joins the group. Woody's egotism and mercenary motive gain him the ill will of his fellow fliers. He further antagonizes the group by trying to steal Jim's girlfriend Brooke (Lee), a Red Cross nurse. He quarrels with one flier, then is blamed for the latter's death in a crash. He fails to be at the base to take off on a special night patrol and the man who takes his place is killed. Woody asks Jim for another chance but he says no.

Jim returns to his desk that morning after the all-night mission, and a close-up of his desk calendar reads December 7, 1941. (In actuality it would have been the morning of December 8, since China is on the other side of the International Date Line). The next scene shows all the fliers listening to Roosevelt's address to Congress on the radio. This is intercut with views of the nurses listening as well as Chinese people. All are in a somber and reflective mood.

Colonel Claire L. Chenault arrives at base the next morning on a transport plane and after saluting says to Jim, "I don't have to tell you what our entrance into the war means to the Volunteer Group in China."

A special mission allows Woody the chance to redeem himself by saving Jim's life when the plane in which they are bombing a Japanese supply train catches fire. The wounded Woody pushes Jim out of the plane, so he can parachute to safety. Woody, at the controls, dives headlong into the train.

In real life, during the summer of 1941, 300 young men and women secretly trained in the jungles of southeast Asia, preparing to face the Japanese Air Force in combat over the skies of China and Burma. Within weeks of the Japanese attack on Pearl Harbor, their heroic exploits captured the American imagination as the Flying Tigers. For years after the Flying Tigers' disbanding in 1942, they were widely thought to be a mercenary air force in the service of the Chinese government. In July of 1991 the United States government belatedly admitted the truth: The Flying Tigers had been created by secret order of President Franklin Roosevelt. Months before Pearl Harbor the Flying Tigers had been created to help the Chinese defend their cities from relentless bombing by the Japanese, who had invaded China in 1937.

The group's members had been recruited from within the ranks of the U.S. Armed Forces. Pilots, aircraft mechanics, propeller specialists, doctors, nurses, clerks and even a chaplain joined what was called the American Volunteer Group. They signed a one-year contract to protect the only supply route open for the United States to deliver war material to China, the Burma Road. They boarded ships from the West Coast in the spring and summer of 1941 traveling as missionaries, planters and circus performers. Their disguises were meant to mask their true mission and protect FDR's secret effort to keep China from falling to the Japanese, without provoking a war with Japan.

BATAAN

MGM, 1943

D: Tay Garnett

S: Robert Andrews

P: Irving Starr

Cast: Robert Taylor, Thomas Mitchell, George Murphy, Lloyd Nolan, Desi Arnaz, Robert Walker

Robert Taylor stars as Sgt. Bill Dane, who leads a group of your typical assortment of representative Americans. Their mission is to stop the advancing Japanese from using a bridge during the Japanese invasion of the Philippines right after Pearl Harbor. The film opens with a fairly graphic scene (for the time) showing the bombing of fleeing troops and civilians and the consequences of that bombing.

SO PROUDLY WE HAIL

Paramount, 1943

D: Mark Sandrich

S: Allan Scott

P: Mark Sandrich

Cast: Claudette Colbert, Paulette Goddard, Veronica Lake

The story, which is told in flashback, opens by introducing a group of Army nurses headed by Claudette Colbert who are aboard a transport bound for Hawai'i. En route, they learn of the Pearl Harbor attack. Their ship changes its course and joins a convoy bound for the Philippines. This was the first Hollywood WWII film to focus on women as nurses at the frontlines.

THE FIGHTING SEABEES

Republic, 1944

D: Edward Ludwig

S: Borden Chase and Aeneas MacKenzie

P: Albert J. Cohen

Cast: John Wayne, Susan Hayward, Dennis O'Keefe, William Frawley

This fictionalized account examines the origins of the famed U.S. Construction Battalion, a military construction force trained to fight as well as build. Wayne plays a civilian contractor who chafes under the military discipline imposed by Naval Officer Lt. Yarrow, played by Dennis O'Keefe. They are both rivals for the affections of Connie (Hayward), a newspaperwoman. Wedge Donovan (Wayne), a top civilian contractor, goes to the docks of San Francisco to meet one of his gangs just back from the South Pacific, where he finds many have been hurt and wounded. He proposes to the Navy the setting up of construction battalions. The plan is approved but Wedge backs down when he finds out the amount of military training his men will have to take. Back in the Pacific, Wedge finds Connie the victim of a Japanese bullet. Sobered by the realities of war conditions, Wedge goes back to Washington and agrees to Navy regulations. He is commissioned and the Construction Battalions (abbreviated to C.B. or "Seabees") are formed.

The film contains a song, *Song of the Seabees,* with music by Peter De Rose and lyrics by Sam M. Lewis which helped boost morale and promoted the organization.

> "We're the Seabees of the Navy
> We can build and we can fight
> We'll pave our way to victory
> And guard it day and night
> And we promise that we'll remember
> The Seventh of December
> We're the Seabees of the Navy
> Bees of the Seven Seas."

Filmed in 1943 at Port Hueneme, Point Mugu and Camp Pendleton, California, the film's release in 1944 made the Seabees a household word. The picture also began a relationship between John Wayne and the Seabees that lasted for more than three decades, ending with what was "The Duke's" last production: *Home for the Seabees,* a documentary filmed in 1977 at the Naval Construction Battalion Center in Port Hueneme, California.

Some of the film's heroic actions actually happened. Aurelio Tassone, a 28-year-old ex-state road builder and bulldozer operator, performed one of the most ingenious heroic feats. During the Treasury Island landing in the Solomons, he roared down the ramp of an LST in his 20-ton bulldozer to attack a Japanese sniper in a coconut-log pillbox, using the steel blade of the bulldozer as a shield and destroying his target with sand and dirt.

The Pacific Seabees built 111 major airstrips, 441 piers, 2,558 ammunition magazines, 700 square blocks of warehouses, gasoline storage tanks, hospitals to serve 70,000 patients, and housing for 1.5 million men. The Pacific Seabees suffered more than 200 deaths and earned more than 200 Purple Hearts. Eighty percent of the Seabees served in the Pacific Theater of war, due to the nature of the island-hopping campaigns in the vast area of the Pacific.

1. At Republic studios, Dennis O'Keefe and John Wayne stand in front of a rear-projection background image screen in order to complete a close-up scene for the film *The Fighting Seabees*.

Luis Reyes Collection

Luis Reyes Collection

2. A scene showing the USS *Juneau* under attack and the resultant tragedy of the loss of the five Sullivan brothers. In reality, two of the brothers were already serving in the Navy at the time of the Pearl Harbor attack, though this is portrayed otherwise in the movie, which shows all five brothers rushing to the recruiting office right after the news of Pearl Harbor. The eldest brother, George, did survive the explosion and sinking of the ship, but after a few days on a raft, he perished during a shark attack.

THE FIGHTING SULLIVANS

aka THE SULLIVANS

Twentieth Century Fox, 1944

D: Lloyd Bacon

S: Mary C. McCall Jr.

P: Sam Jaffe

Cast: Anne Baxter, Thomas Mitchell, Ward Bond, Selena Royle, Edward Ryan, Trudy Marshall

The Fighting Sullivans, inspiring and influencing Spielberg's *Saving Private Ryan* (1998), is the story of five brothers serving aboard the USS *Juneau* during World War II in the South Pacific. All perish when their ship is torpedoed. The latter film deals with an American patrol of Normandy, just after D-Day, who are assigned to find the last surviving brother of a family who have been killed in service to their country.

The Sullivans were George, Francis, Joseph, Madison and Albert. Ranging in age from 20 to 27, they joined the Navy in December 1941 and, against recommendations, insisted on serving on the same ship. On November 13, 1942, during the Battle of Guadalcanal, their vessel was hit by a Japanese torpedo.

Hundreds of sailors died in the Battle of Guadalcanal that day but the deaths of the Sullivan brothers from Waterloo, Iowa, created a navy legend.

The film, which runs 112 minutes, is essentially in three acts. The bulk of the story depicts the brothers as kids and then as adults before the bombing of Pearl Harbor is announced.

THEY WERE EXPENDABLE

MGM, 1945

D: John Ford

S: Frank Wead

P: John Ford

Cast: Robert Montgomery, John Wayne, Donna Reed, Jack Holt, Ward Bond, Cameron Mitchell, Paul Langton

Lt. John Brickley (Montgomery) is having trouble getting his superior officers to see the military value of his new PT craft. Even his friend, Lt. JG "Rusty" Ryan (Wayne) is desperate to transfer to a more exciting unit until the Japanese bomb Pearl Harbor. Suddenly, the Navy needs to send its men to the Philippines. Brickley, Ryan and their little PT fleet are headed for Bataan, right in harm's way with virtually no naval support.

Montgomery came to this production after serving a four-year hitch in the U.S. Navy, and this was Director John Ford's first civilian effort after serving with the Navy as well. Frank Wead, ex-Navy man turned screenwriter (whose credits include *Hell Divers*, *Ceiling Zero*, and *Test Pilot)*, wrote the script based on the non-fiction book *They Were Expendable* by William L. White. It chronicled the exploits of Vice Admiral John D. Bulkeley (1911-1996) and his torpedo-boat squadron (the predecessor of the Navy PT boats in which future U.S. President JFK also served) in the Philippines. In the movie Robert Montgomery played Admiral Bulkeley, who was renamed Brickley in the film.

This was a somewhat curious film to make in 1945. The story is about an early defeat, and at the time the war was still raging, though victory seemed assured by then. The title is a bitter reference to the men who were left behind in the scramble to flee the Philippines after the Japanese invasion. The actions of these men are understated as they carry out their orders and accept this decision which leaves them to face death or imprisonment.

Until Pearl Harbor, the PT boats squadroned at Manila Bay were regarded by complacent officers as little more than pleasure craft. The war suddenly gave the torpedo boats a new and important significance. These tiny high-powered wooden crafts, equipped with guns and torpedo tubes, could slip into enemy-infested waters under cover of night, sink a vessel or two and streak out before being discovered. The PT boats got an opportunity to prove their resourcefulness when the Philippines were blockaded after the Pearl Harbor attack.

BACK TO BATAAN

RKO, 1945

D: Edward Dmytryk

S: Ben Barzman and Richard H. Landau

P: Robert Fellows

Cast: John Wayne, Anthony Quinn, Fely Franqueli, Richard Loo, Philip Ahn

Colonel Joseph Madden (Wayne) is ordered to go to the Luzon hills to organize native guerillas, and, in need of a patriot around whom to rally the men, he rescues Andres Bonifacio (Quinn) from the Japanese. Thinking his sweetheart is aiding the enemy by her frequent broadcasts, Andres is embittered and proves ineffectual until Madden tells him that his girlfriend is actually aiding the resistance movement secretly. Inspired, Andres agrees to lend his support. Under Madden's leadership, the guerillas step up their campaign against the enemy and mount an attack to prepare the way for the American troops by securing a beachhead. Ironically, in this feature, right-winger Duke Wayne was directed by Edward Dmytryk, who two years later would be blacklisted as one of the Hollywood 10.

AN AMERICAN GUERRILLA IN THE PHILIPPINES

Twentieth Century Fox, 1950

D: Fritz Lang

S: Lamar Trotti based on the novel by Ira Wolfert

P: Lamar Trotti

Cast: Tyrone Power, Micheline Presle, Tom Ewell

Tyrone Power is a Naval officer whose ship is sunk off Leyte, and who joins with other stranded Americans to help Filipinos organize their resistance campaign against the Japanese invaders. Lamar Trotti also wrote *To the Shores of Tripoli* and *Guadalcanal Diary*. This was filmed on location in the Philippines.

BATTLE AT BLOODY BEACH

Twentieth Century Fox, 1961

D: Herbert Coleman

S: Richard Maibaum and Willard Willigham
from a story by Maibaum

P: Richard Maibaum

Cast: Audie Murphy, Gary Crosby, Dolores
Michaels, Alejandro Rey, Miriam Colon

It is World War II in the Philippines. A civilian, Craig Benson (Murphy), working with the guerillas, is intent on locating the wife from whom he became separated while honeymooning in Manila when the Japanese struck. This film was made on location in the Philippines.

NO MAN IS AN ISLAND

Universal, 1962

D: John Monks Jr., Richard Goldstone

S: John Monks Jr. And Richard Goldstone

P: John Monks Jr., Richard Goldstone

Cast: Jeffrey Hunter, Marshall Thompson,
Barbara Perez

This is based on the true story of U.S. Navy radioman George Tweed (Hunter) who evaded capture while isolated for 31 months on Guam in the first years of World War II, while the Japanese placed a price on his head. Tweed alerted the U.S. fleet to the positions of the Japanese defenses and task forces on the island. It was made entirely on location in the Philippines, which doubled for Guam.

CRY OF BATTLE

Allied Artists, 1963

D: Irving Lerner

S: Bernard Gordon

P: Joe Steinberg

C: James MacArthur, Rita Moreno, Van Heflin,
Leopoldo Salcedo, Sydney Clute

Cry of Battle opens with Imperial planes swooping down and bombing U.S. aircraft while a title reads: "The Philippines, 12:05 p.m., December 8, 1941." James MacArthur (*Hawaiʻi Five-O*'s Dano and the son of Helen Hayes, the first lady of the American stage) plays Davey MacVeigh, son of a Yankee plantation owner, who's attacked by what seem to be Filipino bandits in this harrowing opening sequence. He's rescued by Filipino guerrillas led by Major Manuel Careo (Leopoldo Salcedo), who hide him in the nipa hut of a local father and his young daughter. The underground also stashes Joe (Van Heflin), a burly seaman who worked for MacVeigh senior on a freighter sunk by the Japanese in Manila Harbor.

The sailor thinks that by taking care of his boss' son, he'll eventually be rewarded. "King Joe" is a racist and sexist who repays the hospitality—not to mention risk—of his Filipino hosts by raping the virginal teenager daughter. Davey is infuriated, but when the girl starts to scream, he joins Joe and they run away into the jungle. The Yanks eventually hook up with Colonel Ryker's American unit, which cooperates with Careo's indigenous freedom fighters. When Joe refers to Filipinos as "geeks" (not gooks), Ryker objects, and Joe replies in a patronizing way. "You can drop that too. They don't want to be loved. They want to be treated like equals. Because that's what they are," Ryker snaps back.

Davey and Joe become part of the resistance, along with a band that includes the sizzling Cesa (Rita Moreno, who won the Best Supporting Actress Oscar for 1961's *West Side Story*). They ambush a Japanese column, and are repulsed. Ryker promotes Joe and entrusts him with an important mission. It turns out Cesa's comrades are part guerrilla, part bandit, and along with Joe, they massacre residents of a local village. Davey condemns Cesa for spending the night with their leader, Joe, and she responds: "You're also a whore," because Joe has saved Davey's life, and continues to protect the rich man's son. In a sensuous love scene straight out of

Opposite page: On the same day that Japan attacked Pearl Harbor, the Japanese also invaded Guam, launching an attack from nearby Saipan, located in the Japanese Mandate isles north of Guam. Japan occupied the U.S. territory until 1944 and, during this time, U.S. serviceman George Tweed (Jeffrey Hunter plays the real-life World War II hero) hid from the Japanese forces with the assistance of Guam's indigenous people, the Chamorros. Here, Tweed embraces his Chamorro girlfriend, played by Barbara Perez, in *No Man is an Island.*

South Seas Cinema, Moreno swims topless in a river near a rice paddy with Davey, and then leaves Joe for the younger, more handsome man.

Colonel Ryker is killed, and Major Careo emerges as the leader of the opposition. He places Joe, Davey, and Cesa under detention in a nipa hut, and urges Davey to sign a statement condemning Joe for his rape and pillage. But out of misplaced loyalty, Davey declines to do so. Japanese invade the village where they're being held, and Davey uses a lantern as a Molotov cocktail to set a tank on fire. The trio escape and live near the sea. Joe, who's been wounded, pretends to be weaker than he really is, and Davey and Cesa take care of him. Joe calls Cesa a "chippie," and tells Davey, "You've forgotten you're a white man." When Davey's away, Joe seduces Cesa, and Davey beats Joe, who refuses to fight over a mere Filipina.

While Major Coreo leads a beach patrol, Joe knocks Davey down, shoots a guerrilla in the back, and tries to kill Coreo. But Davey's had enough—Dan books 'em as Davey, shoots and kills Joe. The freedom fighter asks Davey, "Do you want to join us?"

The black-and-white, low-budget *Cry of Battle* was shot entirely on location in the Philippines and used Filipino cast and crew. It is an offbeat action film with an indie sensibility, written by blacklisted Hollywood screenwriter Bernard Gordon (who also wrote the scripts for 1963's *55 Days at Peking*, 1965's *Battle of the Bulge*, 1968's *Custer of the West*, 1969's *Krakatoa, East of Java*, and 1964's *The Thin Red Line*, which follows the exploits of the *Eternity* infantrymen at Guadalcanal). As with Lester Cole's screenplay for *Blood on the Sun*, *Cry* is an example of how leftist writers put progressive politics into scripts. Gordon was a longtime Communist Party member, a fact reflected in the script's preoccupation with guerrilla warfare, anti-racism, depiction of a woman bearing arms, and interracial romance theme. Tellingly, *Cry*'s most dignified character by far is not white, but rather Major Coreo (played by a Filipino), the underground leader. Davey's refusal to inform on Joe reflects the fact that Gordon, like other Tinseltown progressives, refused to be "friendly witnesses" for the HUAC witchhunters. (In his 1999 autobiography, *Hollywood Exile, or How I Learned to Love the Blacklist*, Gordon reveals that using a pseudonym, he wrote 1957's Guam-set *Hellcats of the Navy*, the only flick pairing Ronald Reagan and Nancy Davis.

MACARTHUR

Universal, 1977

D: Joseph Sargent

S: Hal Barwood and Matthew Robbins

P: Frank McCarthy

Cast: Gregory Peck, Ed Flanders, Dan O'Herlihy

This biopic about the controversial general and would-be politician Douglas MacArthur (Gregory Peck) covers nearly a decade, from the Imperial offensive against the Philippines to President Truman's 1951 dismissal of MacArthur during the Korean War. The saga is bookended by MacArthur's famous farewell speech to cadets at his beloved West Point in 1961, wherein he poetically told the long gray line: "old soldiers never die… they just fade away." From West Point, the film flashbacks to a title: "Corregidor, The Philippines, 1942," followed by another title stating, "Three Months After The Japanese Attack On Pearl Harbor," superimposed over wounded Yanks and Filipinos, who enter a makeshift hospital inside a tunnel.

The film follows the Supreme Commander of the Southwest Area as he reluctantly flees his beloved Philippines with his wife (Sandy Kenyon) and son on a PT boat to assume command in Australia. He goes on to lead a Big Mac attack of then-New Guinea, as the Allies invade the Japanese-held island. Afterwards, his flies to Pearl Harbor for a high-level powwow with FDR (Dan O'Herlihy), Admiral Nimitz, et al, and debates strategy for the Pacific's island-hopping campaign. MacArthur prevails, and instead of Formosa the Allies launch an amphibious invasion of the Philippines, which Mac watches with the President of the Philippines, and is intercut onscreen with color newsreel footage.

In a carefully choreographed moment, the media-savvy General keeps his promise, wading ashore from a troop transport and declares: "People of the Philippines, I have returned… The hour of your redemption is near." In a live radio broadcast, Mac also urges Filipino guerrillas to "Strike!" As Luzon is liberated, MacArthur encounters those who stayed behind and survived: suffering, emaciated Filipino prisoners and emaciated survivors of the horrific Bataan Death March. As the masses adore him, the General ruefully comments, "I finally returned, but a little late."

1.MacArthur (Gregory Peck) adds his signature to history at the Japanese surrender aboard the battleship USS *Missouri*. This scene was filmed on the actual deck of the historic ship where the surrender took place. The USS *Missouri* is now permanently anchored at Pearl Harbor.

1

2.The quarterdeck of the USS *Missouri* is the site for the re-enactment of the signing of the Japanese surrender ceremonies which ended World War II in this scene from *MacArthur,* starring Gregory Peck as general of the Army Douglas MacArthur.

2

FDR dies; Truman is briefed about the atomic bomb and nukes Hiroshima and Nagasaki, outraging MacArthur, who wanted to invade the Imperial homeland. Cut to the USS *Missouri* in Tokyo Bay, on September 2, 1945, as MacArthur leads the signing ceremony that officially ends the Second World War. Representatives of Japan and the various Allies sign the document. MacArthur magnanimously gives General Jonathan Wainwright—who remained in the P.I. and, against Mac's wishes, surrendered to the Imperial invaders—a pen for him to add his signature. This sequence was filmed on the actual USS *Missouri*, which is now permanently located in Pearl Harbor.

In a moving sequence, as black-and-white newsreel footage of a destroyed Japanese city is shown, MacArthur is heard stating: "I pray that an omnipotent providence will summon all good persons to the realization of the utter futility of war." As the camera pans to the Soviets aboard the *Missouri*, Mac adds, "War, the most malignant scourge and greatest sin of mankind, can no longer be controlled, only abolished. We are in a new era. If we do not devise some greater, more equitable means of settling disputes between nations, Armageddon will be at our door. We have had our last chance."

Mac heads the occupation of Japan. He retains Hirohito on his throne, and institutes a New Deal in Japan, with land reform, labor and women's movements, aimed at breaking the power of right-wing industrialists and landowners. When the Korean War erupts, the anti-communist General again heads for the front. Mac disagrees with Truman's policies and wants to expand the war. They meet to parley at Midway, where the General keeps his Commander In Chief waiting, and

Truman goes on to sack MacArthur. His political ambitions remain unfulfilled, as the old general fades away after his West Point speech.

Peck portrays MacArthur as a Lord Jim wannabe, full of hubris and vainglorious preening for the cameras. Nonetheless, the film is curiously flat and stilted, lacking the verve and panache of that other 1970s WWII biopic, George C. Scott's *Patton*. Most of *MacArthur* was filmed on locations in and around Los Angeles.

1941

Universal, 1979

D: Steven Spielberg

S: Robert Zemeckis and Bob Gale from a story by John Milius

P: John Milius

Cast: Dan Aykroyd, John Belushi, Tim Matheson, Robert Stack, Toshiro Mifune, Ned Beatty

This wacky look at the homefront is sort of *It's A Mad Mad Mad Mad World* meets *The Russians Are Coming! The Russians Are Coming!* meets *Tora!*

Ornery American lumberjack Hollis Wood (Slim Pickens) is interrogated aboard a Japanese submarine in *1941*. Pickens also took a wild ride aboard a nuclear bomb in Stanley Kubrick's *Dr. Strangelove*.

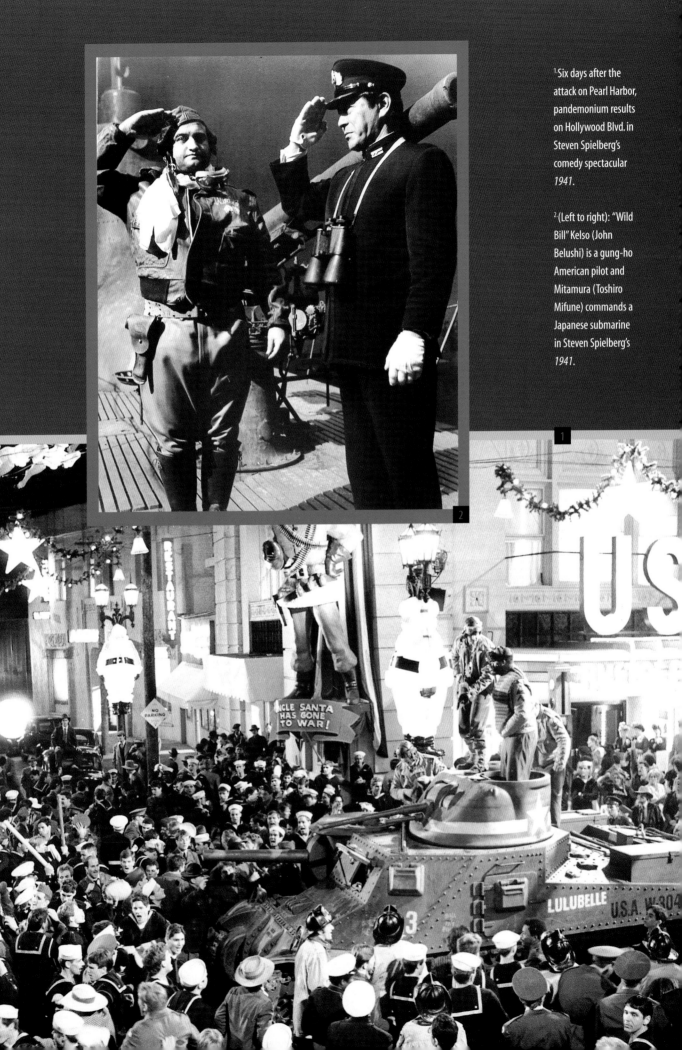

1. Six days after the
attack on Pearl Harbor,
pandemonium results
on Hollywood Blvd. in
Steven Spielberg's
comedy spectacular
1941.

2. (Left to right): "Wild
Bill" Kelso (John
Belushi) is a gung-ho
American pilot and
Mitamura (Toshiro
Mifune) commands a
Japanese submarine
in Steven Spielberg's
1941.

1

2

Tora! Tora! meets *Animal House*, and could've been called "Toga! Toga! Toga!" *1941* reunites the frat brothers John Belushi and Tim Matheson, and was originally going to be a small comedy film written and directed by John Milius (*Conan The Barbarian*, *Apocalypse Now*). It was turned into a large-scale production for Steven Spielberg following the success of *Close Encounters of the Third Kind*.

The film is set in Los Angeles during the panic-stricken days following the attack on Pearl Harbor, when most of the population of Southern California believed that a Japanese invasion could come at any time. Those fears lead to "The Great Los Angeles Air Raid." On February 22, 1942, for almost 45 minutes the Los Angeles area sky turned into one huge pyrotechnic display. The antiaircraft guns began exploding at 3:12 a.m. with searchlights scanning the skies. Reported sightings of enemy aircraft came in from all over the city. Defensive shrapnel rained down, causing damage to houses. But no bombs were dropped and no planes were downed, and once the shooting had died down it had to be admitted that the whole thing had been a false alarm, triggered by panic and a weather balloon. Two days earlier a Japanese submarine had shelled an oil refinery north of Santa Barbara.

Spielberg remarked in the film's production notes, "This is a comedy, not a war picture. We've bent history like a pretzel."

SWING SHIFT
Warner Brothers, 1984

D: Jonathan Demme

S: Rob Morten

P: Arlene Sellers and Alex Winitsky

Cast: Goldie Hawn, Kurt Russell, Christine Lahti, Ed Harris, Fred Ward

It is a tender and emotional story about the women and the men who back at the homefront went to work in the factories for war production. As more and more men were being called into the armed forces, woman were needed at the assembly-line plants in order to produce the weapons of war. The experience of war on the homefront and on the battlefield changed the social conditions of both women and men in the U.S. and brought on social changes that would reverberate for years to come.

The film begins on December 6 introducing the characters. Kay (Hawn) and Jack (Harris) are a young married couple skating at a roller rink on the Santa Monica Beach pier on Sunday, December 7. The radio announcement from one of the booths is brief and dramatic; the Japanese have just bombed Pearl Harbor. The film dramatized the fear and uncertainty facing those who lived on the West Coast.

EMPIRE OF THE SUN
Amblin Entertainment, 1987

D: Steven Spielberg

S: Tom Stoppard

P: Steven Spielberg, Kathleen Kennedy, Frank Marshall

C: John Malkovich, Miranda Richardson, Christian Bale, Ben Stiller, Joe Pantoliano, Takatoro Kataoka, Russell Crowe

The narrator and opening titles of this largely made-in-China epic explain that the Japanese and Chinese have been fighting an undeclared war for four years. "In Shanghai, Westerners, protected by diplomatic security, continued to live as they had in their own country. Now their time was running out. Outside Shanghai the Japanese dug in and waited… for Pearl Harbor." Jamie Grey (Christian Bale) is the spoiled son of a privileged British family, growing up in the milieu of expat Shanghai. He is fixated on the Zero fighter plane, and has a toy model of one. Jamie and the upper-crust circle he moves in are rude and racist to Asians, and detached from the misery most Chinese live in.

Of course, when the Imperial troops do invade Shanghai (starting December 8, 1941, Shanghai time), they are just as cruel—if not more so—than the Westerners. During the invasion, Jamie is separated from his parents in all of the chaos. He falls in with some Yank and ends up in an internment camp. Unlike the AJAs in *Come See the Paradise* and *Midway*, in Shanghai it is "whitey" who is interned—and in far more brutal conditions.

Jamie does what it takes to get by in the camp as a wheeler-dealer. This child of the elite is sometimes so irritating and bratty that you hope the camp commandant will behead him with a samurai sword. But in the end, you can't help but admire Jamie—he's a parentless child lost in the upheavals of war who has come down in the world, yet he's a real survivor.

Empire of the Sun is based on the autobiographical novel by J.G. Ballard, is distributed by Warners, and has music composed by John Williams. Along with *1941*, *Schindler's List*, and *Saving Private Ryan*, this is at least the fourth feature by Steven Spielberg about WWII (his father was a D-Day veteran).

Russell Crowe, who won the Best Actor Oscar for 2000's *Gladiator*, had his movie debut in *Empire* as a British officer.

RADIO DAYS

Orion, 1987

D: Woody Allen
S: Woody Allen
P: Robert Greenhut

Cast: Mia Farrow, Seth Green, Julie Kavner, Josh Mostel, Michael Tucker, Dianne Wiest

Luis Reyes Collection

Woody Allen is the poet laureate of New York Jews. His 15th film consists of a boy's childhood memories of growing up in Far Rockaway, N.Y. listening to the radio for entertainment and escape, as so many Americans did. Set at the start of World War II, it's a world of aunts and uncles all living on top of each other and the magical events and people, real and imagined, that forever shape one's young imagination. Allen narrates the film from the boy's point of view, but never appears in it—the lad is obviously Woody's alter ego. The witty story seamlessly weaves together a running commentary on some half-dozen odd characters, including both his Jewish family and the denizens of high society of New York.

In one hilarious scene, Sally (Mia Farrow) is about to make her long-awaited radio debut by lending her Brooklyn accent to a Chekhov play. Just as Sally is about to speak, though, an announcer bursts into the studio and preempts the wannabe thespian, breaking the news that Pearl Harbor has been bombed. Sally is miffed that she's been cut off, and the ditzy blonde asks: "Who is Pearl Harbor?" With disappointment she observes, "There's always other girls horning in on your big break."

Mia Farrow as seen in Woody Allen's comedy *Radio Days*. Farrow is the daughter of film director John Farrow, who directed *Wake Island,* and she was married briefly to Frank Sinatra. She was also married to film director Woody Allen and appeared in several of his films. They are now divorced.

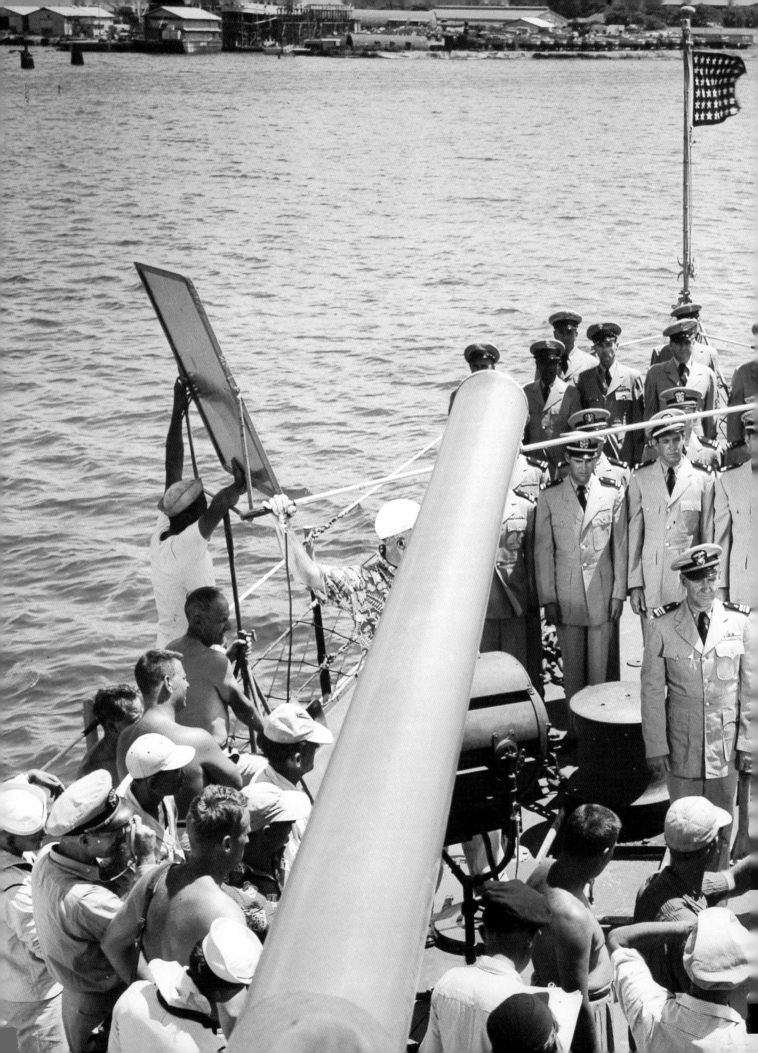

CHAPTER 4
Pearl Harbor
in the Movies

PEARL HARBOR IN THE MOVIES

ON DECEMBER 7, 1941, the name Pearl Harbor was emblazoned in the hearts and minds of most Americans, forever etched on the geographic map of the American consciousness. Hundreds of thousands of American soldiers, sailors and Marines got their first glimpse of Hawai'i and the fabled South Pacific on their way to the Pacific theater of war. It was the first time many had ever been away from home, let alone transported clear across the world.

James Jones, James Michener, William Bradford Huie and Herman Wouk wrote about their wartime experiences in popular novels that were made into movies.

In a short time, Midway, Guadalcanal, Tarawa, the Solomons, Saipan, and Iwo Jima would become household words that signified victories, but at a terrible human cost.

Popular Hollywood images were so pervasive that upon landing on a Japanese-held Pacific island, a Marine remarked, "Where's Dorothy Lamour in her sarong?" During the bombing of Pearl, one serviceman commented that it looked just like a movie set.

There are a number of motion pictures in which Pearl Harbor and Honolulu-type environments figure prominently in the story lines. These movies can take the form of prewar service comedies or romances (*Wings Over Honolulu*, *Here Comes the Navy*, *In the Navy*); action war dramas (*Sands of Iwo Jima*, *Gung Ho*, *Operation Pacific*, *Torpedo Run*); instructional service dramas (*Wing and a Prayer*, *Task Force*, *Away All Boats*); and post war dramas (*Big Jim McLain*, *Court Martial Of Billy Mitchell*, *Hell to Eternity*, *Crimson Tide*).

These films use Pearl Harbor as a pro-active place for orders through Naval headquarters, a refuge for repairs after battle engagements and as a Shangri-La for R&R (rest and recreation). It is also the first place for disembarkation from the continental U.S. mainland on the way to forward Pacific battle areas.

It is a last glimpse of an exotic version of America before they are confronted with the harsh, grim realities of the battlefield and their rite of manhood under fire.

A parade of assorted characters is portrayed in these films: career naval officers, daring aviators, hardened seasoned veterans, nurses, raw recruits and a collage of regional or ethnic types all representative of America.

The postwar years offered dramas that more closely examined America's role in the war, both on the battlefield and on the homefront. Some of these films touched on subjects including the need for vigilance and the Communist threat. Others told true personal stories like that of a courageous proponent of early military aviation who predicted the Pearl Harbor attack 17 years before it happened, and a Mexican-American war hero, raised by a Japanese-American family interned by Executive Order 9066.

These movies solidified Pearl Harbor's image in the public mind as a bastion of America's Naval force in the Pacific to the present day.

THE FLYING FLEET

MGM, 1929

D: George Hill

C: Ramon Novarro, Ralph Graves, Anita Page

Navy pilots attempt a flight from California to Hawai'i but have to ditch at sea. Two versions, one silent and the other synchronized. Courtesy Robert C. Schmitt, *Hawaii in the Movies, 1898-1959*, Hawai'i Historical Society, 1988.

LEATHERNECKING

RKO, 1930

D: Edward Cline

C: Irene Dunn, Ken Murray, Louise Fazenda, Ned Sparks, Lilyan Tashman

A Marine private stationed in Honolulu unsuccessfully tries to impress the daughter of an English nobleman/planter but is exposed. Maneuvered aboard a mutual friend's yacht, the two are marooned on an island inhabited by "savage belles." Rescued, they return to Honolulu, where the marine is put in the brig but is eventually reunited with the planter's daughter. Released in September 12, 1930, *Leathernecking* is noted mostly for its use of color film (for 20 minutes of its 72-minute running time) and its music by Richard Rodgers and Lorenz Hart, making it both the first color feature and first musical in Hawai'i's movie history. Courtesy Robert C. Schmitt, *Hawaii in the Movies, 1898-1959*, Hawai'i Historical Society, 1988.

FLIRTATION WALK

First National/Warner Bros., 1934

D: Frank Borzage

C: Dick Powell, Ruby Keeler, Pat O'Brien

A musical set in Schofield Barracks, Waikīkī, and West Point, O'ahu, Hawai'i. Courtesy Robert C. Schmitt, *Hawaii in the Movies, 1898-1959*, Hawai'i Historical Society, 1988.

HERE COMES THE NAVY

Warner Bros, 1934

D: Lloyd Bacon

S: Ben Markson and Earl Baldwin

P: Lou Edelman

C: James Cagney, Pat O'Brien, Gloria Stuart, Dorothy Tree, Frank McHugh, Guinn Williams

James Cagney plays a cocky shipyard proletarian named Chesty who gets into a spat at the job site with Pat O'Brien, a Naval officer named Biff. The rivalry deepens when Biff publicly steals Chesty's girlfriend at a dance and then beats him up. The ironworker enlists in the prewar Navy for the sole purpose of getting stationed on Biff's ship so he can get even. Sure enough, courtesy of Uncle Sam, Chesty is billeted on Biff's battleship—the West Coast-stationed USS *Arizona*, where part of this comedy-drama was actually filmed. Then, Chesty falls in love with Gloria Stuart (who'd much later appear in another film about a famous ship, The *Titanic*)—who just so happens to be Biff's kid sister. Complications ensue.

Chesty goes AWOL to see his sweetheart by disguising himself in blackface as the African-American sailor Cookie. He bamboozles the *Arizona*'s officers and goes ashore with a group of black sailors enjoying liberty. Chesty shocks Gloria Stuart when she sees him in blackface, and in turn

HERE COMES THE NAVY

[1] James Cagney and Pat O'Brien were cast for the first time as friendly adversaries in *Here Comes the Navy*. The girl in question was Gloria Stuart, better known to contemporary audiences as the actress who played the old woman in the film *Titanic*. The movie was filmed on the USS *Arizona* in 1934, seven years before its fateful date with infamy.

[2] James Cagney, Pat O'Brien, Gloria Stuart and Allen Jenkins in *Here Comes the Navy*.

the African-American sailors stare at Chesty in this racially insensitive scene.

Although he's undisciplined, Chesty has courage, and is injured when he swiftly puts out a gunpowder fire onboard the *Arizona* during artillery practice. The Secretary of the Navy awards Chesty the Navy Cross, but he disses the medal. He is transferred to an aircraft unit and defends the gobs of the *Arizona* to the dirigible crew. During a blimp exercise, Chesty rescues Biff in a daring parachute jump. In the final scene, Biff is in crutches, Chesty in a wheelchair, as he marries Gloria Stuart. A presidential proclamation promotes Chesty.

Here Comes the Navy was the first of eight films Cagney was to make with O'Brien, and the first of his three Pearl-related pictures.

WINGS OVER HONOLULU

Universal, 1937

D: H.C. Potter

S: Isabel Dawn and Boyce DeGaw

P: Charles I. Rogers

Cast: Wendy Barrie, Ray Milland, Kent Taylor

The story of a southern belle who marries a Navy flyer and her difficulties in adjusting to life in Honolulu, where her husband has been stationed.

DIVE BOMBER

Warner Bros., 1941

D: Michael Curtiz

S: Frank W. Wead and Robert Buckner

P: Robert Lord

Cast: Errol Flynn, Fred MacMurray, Ralph Bellamy, Alexis Smith

Lt. Douglas Lee (Flynn) a Navy doctor, meets Comdr. Joe Blake (MacMurray) at a Naval hospital in Hawai'i. A conflict between the two men begins when Lee is unable to save the life of one of Blake's buddies, an air crash victim. Lee transfers to San Diego where he can work with a leading specialist in Naval medicine.

NAVY BLUES

Warner Bros., 1941

D: Lloyd Bacon

S: Sam Perrin, Jerry Wald, Richard Macaulay and Arthur T. Horman

P: Hal B. Wallis and Jerry Wald

Cast: Ann Sheridan, Jack Oakie, Martha Raye, Jack Haley, Jack Carson, Jackie Gleason

Pearl Harbor and Honolulu figure prominently in this musical service comedy about the misadventures of a Naval ship's crew that goes on leave in Honolulu. One of the first screen appearances of the celebrated comedian Jackie Gleason, who would find stardom just ten years later as one of the pioneers of the new medium of television in the series *The Honeymooners*.

IN THE NAVY

Universal, 1941

D: Arthur Lubin

S: Arthur T. Horman and John Grant

P: Alex Gottlieb

Cast: Bud Abbott, Lou Costello, Dick Powell, The Andrews Sisters, Shemp Howard

Who's on first? Universal reunited Abbott and Costello with the Andrews Sisters by following the Army comedy *Buck Privates* with another service comedy, *In The Navy*. Bud (Smokey) and Lou

[1] William Gargan, Samuel S. Hinds and Wendy Barrie in a scene from *Wings Over Honolulu*, a prewar Navy love story set in Pearl Harbor, Hawai'i.

[2] Fred MacMurray, Errol Flynn and Ralph Bellamy in the instructional service drama *Dive Bomber*. MacMurray would play a Navy man again years later in *The Caine Mutiny* and Bellamy, alternating between stage and films, would gain a personal artistic triumph with his portrayal of Franklin Delano Roosevelt in both the stage and film versions of *Sunrise at Campobello*.

(Pomeroy) are bus drivers who join the prewar Navy with Dick Powell (Russ), a crooner who opens the comedy singing *Anchors Aweigh* on a live radio broadcast. There is a star-stalking subplot, as the bobbysoxers' teen idol disappears—he's surreptitiously joined the Navy, where a paparazzi female photographer, Dot, pursues Russ in order to sell photos of the recruit to the tabloid press. (Shades of Princess Diana!) The new sailors are shipped out to what Patti Andrews calls "Hawaya" aboard the USS *Alabama* (probably an allusion to the USS *Arizona*…) En route, Pomeroy is befuddled by hammocks in a typical Bud and Lou slapstick scene (don't try this one at home, kiddies!), and there are sight gags, such as oversized boxer shorts. Smokey conducts a big band aboard the battleship. The number Russ croons includes the lyrics: "We're in the Navy, watchdogs of liberty… We're the first line of defense."

Stationed on Oʻahu, the swabbies attend an ersatz luʻau, where the chubby Pomeroy eats the peels but tosses the bananas away, and Smokey eats poi with his fingers. On an obvious studio soundstage, accompanied by a Hawaiian band with a steel guitar and hula dancers, the Andrews Sisters, in Aloha Friday attire (with bongo drums around their waists), sing a song called *Hula-Ba-Luau*: "Here is a real Hawaiian treat—with a boogie-woogie beat!"

Although the Naval base where the boys are stationed is never specifically named, it is clearly meant to be Pearl. The denouement of *In the Navy* is psychologically revealing, as it was shot shortly before Zeros wreaked havoc on Pearl Harbor in reality. In a dream sequence no less, Pomeroy pretends he's a captain or admiral in order to impress Patti Andrews. Dressed as a wannabe Horatio Hornblower, he gives the fleet outrageous orders during war games, showing off for visiting politicians and military brass. Smokey is meant to intercept the piped-up orders but doesn't, and artillery is fired, torpedoes stream towards the flagship, airplanes are deployed from ships, and vessels are on collision courses. Of course, the visiting senators and officers think all is well and are duly impressed by this wacky version of the PacRim war games, which fortunately avoid tragedy when Pomeroy awakes from the drug-induced fantasy. Russ and Dot agree to marry, but in reality there would not be a happy ending for Pearl Harbor and the USS *Alabama/Arizona*, nor would the sailors and soldiers be able to wake up from a bad dream and go back to normal routines.

The laughter sticks in one's throat when the viewer realizes that months after this 1941 film was released, a far worse nightmare would be perpetrated, in real life, on the Pearl Harbor Naval Base—it would be war, not games. *In the Navy* may be an unconscious filmic projection of the military's lack of preparedness and competence, and more importantly, a premonition of a hard rain that's about to fall.

TO THE SHORES OF TRIPOLI
Twentieth Century Fox, 1942

D: H. Bruce Humberstone
S: Lamar Trotti
P: Daryl Zanuck
C: John Payne, Randolph Scott, Maureen
O'Hara, Harry Morgan, Alan Hale, Jr.

The title of this feature is, of course, taken from the Marine Corps Hymn, and the film reminds us that the first time Marines set foot on foreign soil was at Tripoli (now ruled by Colonel Qadaffi). Playboy John Payne's father is a World War I vet who arranges for his son to join the Marines and be trained by dad's old WWI comrade, drill sergeant Randolph Scott, in order to make the proverbial man out of him. The wealthy prima donna has trouble adapting to the rigors of boot camp, as the film follows the exploits of the undisciplined Payne and a motley crew of recruits. Payne falls for military nurse Maureen O'Hara, whose uncle is the commanding officer at the San Diego Marine Corps

Luis Rey

Russell Hicks, Maureen O'Hara and John Payne in To The Shores of Tripoli.

Base, where much of this film was shot on location. Payne connives to win O'Hara's love through game-playing and trickery. Meanwhile, during war games, Payne saves Scott's life in a particularly exciting sequence. Nevertheless, Payne wants out of the Corps, and successfully seeks an early discharge.

The relationship between O'Hara (whose hair seems to get redder as this early Technicolor picture progresses) and Payne is painful to watch, it's so imbecilic. It epitomizes the Pearl pictures trend of the (often insipid, petty) personal life confronted by world historical events. Lamar Trotti's script also has a number of revelatory remarks. The sexually repressed O'Hara aptly says: "Maybe I should be psychoanalyzed." And there are many homosexual references, such as when the macho Scott (who according to some accounts was gay) tells his troops: "You men are moving into tents today, so pick yourself a wife." But as unbearable as the private-life saga is, the final five or so minutes of *Tripoli* make up for it.

Having successfully received early retirement from the USMC, Payne is riding in the back of a taxi with his new bimbo when he hears news about the Pearl Harbor raid on a radio. (This may be the granddaddy of that oft-repeated scene.) Payne stops the cab, deserts his new girlfriend, and joins a Marine parade led by Scott which just happens to be passing by. But the sarge refuses to allow the newly cashiered Payne, who's dressed in civilian garb, to join the marching men. "This isn't just your war. I've got as much right as anyone—" Payne protests. Scott points out that Payne is out of uniform, but he removes Marine khakis from a suitcase, and as Payne's marching comrades close ranks about him, strips off his civvies and tosses them into the crowd of onlookers cheering the Marines. At a troop ship, Payne tells his proud veteran father, "I'll send you a couple of Japs for Christmas," as he boards. Of course, waiting for him at the top of the gangway aboard the vessel is the nurse, Maureen O'Hara. The peacetime Marine Corps may be one thing, but the wartime military is quite another. The Pearl Harbor attack rallies Payne, as it did a nation similarly reluctant to get ensnared in the global conflagration. Payne puts aside his pettiness and joins the crusade against fascism, and in the process, earns the respect and approval of his father, lover, sergeant, C.O., and a grateful nation. *Semper fi!*

In addition to its stirring, clever conclusion, *Tripoli* is also noteworthy because, as previously noted, a Fox Movietone cameraman happened to be on location shooting background shots for this feature when the Imperial forces struck at Pearl Harbor. *To the Shores of Tripoli* was part of the commemorative set of 10 Fox videos released in 1991 in order to mark the 50th anniversary of the Battle of O'ahu.

GUNG HO!

Universal, 1943

D: Ray Enright

S: Joseph Hoffman, Lucien Hubbard

P: Walter Wanger

Cast: Randolph Scott, Grace McDonald, Noah Beery Jr., J. Carrol Naish, Robert Mitchum, Rod Cameron

The story of Carlson's Raider's, *Gung Ho!* was a precursor to *The Dirty Dozen* (1967) and *The Devil's Brigade* (1968). Randolph Scott plays a Marine colonel who right after Pearl Harbor is assigned to put together a company of fearless jungle-trained marines for a secret raid on the Japanese-held Makin Island. He recruits his men from the dregs of society. This is a violent, action-packed film.

Makin Island was actually recaptured just a few weeks before the film's release. This was one of the first film roles for future superstar Robert Mitchum. It was filmed at Camp Pendleton Marine Corps base in Oceanside, California, and at Universal Studios' backlot.

WING AND A PRAYER

aka THE STORY OF CARRIER X

Twentieth Century Fox, 1944

D: Henry Hathaway

S: Jerome Cady

P: William A. Bacher and Walter Morosco

Cast: Don Ameche, Charles Bickford, William Eythe, Dana Andrews, Sir Cedric Hardwicke, Richard Jaeckel, Henry Morgan

This is the story of an aircraft carrier and its involvement in the Pacific campaign against the Japanese focusing on a new group of pilots and the tough flight officer who commands their respect.

1. Charles Bickford is flanked by Don Ameche on the right in *Wing And A Prayer* (*The Story of Carrier X*).

2. Men aboard an aircraft carrier just before an attack in *Wing And A Prayer*.

Twentieth Century Fox's construction department was put to the test in making the 36 sets required for *Wing and a Prayer*. In these sets, they recreated an aircraft carrier in its entirety, even duplicating gun turrets with guns that actually fired. Director Henry Hathaway and a film crew spent seven weeks aboard a carrier. They shot 50,000 feet of film and accompanying sound tracks of both operational activities and actual combat.

Since the film was released during the war, for military reasons the carrier, other ships, and individuals were not permitted to be named.

"Where is our Navy?" was the cry heard throughout the land shortly after that fateful day in December 1941. Few people could understand and least of all those aboard Carrier X why an immediate retaliation to the blow against our fleet was not permitted. Strategy, it developed, was behind this delay. The real seriousness of the damage done to our Navy could not be divulged to the enemy.

ON AN ISLAND WITH YOU

MGM, 1948

D: Richard Thorpe

C: Esther Williams, Peter Lawford, Jimmy Durante, Xavier Cougat

A musical about the filming of a South Seas movie in a resort area much like Hawai'i. A Navy lieutenant from a nearby base—serving as a technical consultant to this film within a film—flies the star to an island 500 miles distant where he had met her during the war, and where they are now given a lū'au by the Polynesian inhabitants.

Courtesy Robert C. Schmitt, *Hawaii in the Movies, 1898-1959*, Hawai'i Historical Society, 1988.

SANDS OF IWO JIMA

Republic Pictures, 1949

D: Alan Dwan

S: Harry Brown and James Edward Grant

P: Edmund Grainger

Cast: John Wayne, John Agar, Forrest Tucker, Adele Mara, Wally Cassell, Richard Webb

At Camp Pakakariki in New Zealand in 1943, a squad of raw recruits learn to be Marines from seasoned campaigner Sgt. John M. Stryker (Wayne)

whose ruthless training puts hate into the hearts of his men. His particular enemies are Corporal Thomas (Tucker) and Private Peter Conway (Agar), the son of a Marine officer killed at Guadalcanal. Stryker proves his own courage during the Tarawa campaign and the men come to appreciate the hard lessons he has taught them.

The Marines arrive at Pearl for a short leave before they are shipped out again. Sgt. Stryker (Wayne) meets a woman (Julie Bishop) at a Honolulu nightspot who is a hooker. When they go back to her apartment, Stryker discovers that she has a baby and that her husband had been killed in action. Alone in the Islands, this is the only way she can make a living. Stryker excuses himself and leaves her some money; sparing her dignity, he tells her it's for milk for the baby. (In reality, all military dependents like this woman were evacuated from Hawai'i to the mainland immediately after the attack.)

The squad arrives on Iwo Jima for one of the bloodiest battles in the Pacific war, taking one of the first Japanese home islands. Conway redeems himself in Stryker's eyes and by heroic efforts the island is captured, although Stryker is killed.

The famous photograph and combat film footage of the flag-raising on Mt. Suribachi immortalizes the capture of Iwo Jima by the U.S. Marines. The film uses three of the original soldiers who participated in the actual flag raising: PFCs Rene A. Gagnon and Ira H. Hayes, and PMS/C John H. Bradley. The famous photo of this event was taken by journalist Joe Rosenthal hours after the taking of Mt. Suribachi. It was quickly used by the press in America to show how the Marines were winning the war. Later, a statue was based upon this photograph which caught the public's imagination, making it one of the most famous photos of World War II.

Wayne won an Academy Award nomination as Best Actor for this strong performance that forever associated him in the public's mind in the role of the quintessential American fighting man.

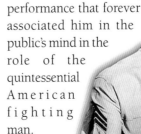

John Wayne received his first Best Actor Oscar nomination for his role as the battle-hardened Sgt. Stryker in the 1949 Marine war drama *Sands of Iwo Jima*. He won a Best Actor Oscar 20 years later for his role as Sheriff Rooster Cogburn in *True Grit*. In this scene he strikes up an acquaintance at a Honolulu bar with a prostitute (Julie Bishop), to whom he reveals glimpses of his past.

TASK FORCE

Warner Bros., 1949

D: Delmer Daves

S: Delmer Daves

P: Jerry Wald

Cast: Gary Cooper, Jane Wyatt, Wayne Morris, Walter Brennan, Stanley Ridges, Bruce Bennett

John Ridgely as Dixie Rankin talks with Gary Cooper as Admiral Jonathan L. Scott at the Flight Operations Bridge just before he takes off for battle in *Task Force.*

This is the story of Naval commander Jonathan L. Scott (Cooper) and his effort to persuade the Navy of the growing importance of aircraft carriers from the 1920s through his retirement in 1949, the beginning of the jet age.

The Pearl Harbor attack sequence combines footage from John Ford's *December 7th* and Warner's own 1943 production of *Air Force*. Scott is at sea on the aircraft carrier *Enterprise* on his way back to Pearl when the attack happens. His wife and two of her friends at Pearl are playing tennis when a Japanese Zero strafes the field; one of the women, who is the wife of Coop's best friend, is killed.

The film was begun in 1945 but was shelved; production resumed in 1948. Producer Jerry Wald and director Delmer Daves culled through over 4 million feet of Navy footage, some from the early days of carrier aviation, and picked out 2,200 feet for the film. When originally released, two-thirds of the film was in black and white and the last third was in color in order to integrate the earlier black-and-white clips with the more recent color World War II footage.

715-85

OPERATION PACIFIC

Warner Bros., Pictures 1951

D: George Waggner

S: George Waggner

P: Louis F. Edelman

Cast: John Wayne, Patricia Neal, Ward Bond, Scott Forbes, Phil Carey, Paul Picerni

The time is 1943. The U.S. Submarine *Thunderfish*, on war patrol, is lying off a Japanese-held island. Commander John T. "Pop" Ferry (Bond) is watching the shoreline through the periscope. Suddenly, crashing out of the jungle comes a strange column headed by Lt. Commander Duke Gifford (Wayne). He is cradling a baby in his arms. Behind him come two nuns helping a number of small children ranging in age from 5 to 10 years. The little group, assisted by several submariners, is taken to the *Thunderfish* in life rafts and boards the sub.

During the run back to Pearl Harbor, the submarine sights several Japanese destroyers and a carrier. As the children whimper in the tense atmosphere, the sub fires all its torpedoes. But through the periscope the submariners see that the torpedoes have exploded prematurely, only halfway to the target. The Japanese destroyers then depth-charge the sub, but it gets away.

Back at Pearl, Duke visits the Naval hospital to see the baby from the island. There he runs into Lt. Mary Stuart (Neal), his ex-wife. It is obvious that Duke and Mary are still in love.

The *Thunderfish* shoves off for another patrol. There is trouble with the torpedoes. The sub attacks an enemy freighter that turns out to be a decoy. Pop is on the bridge of the surfaced sub when the decoy opens fire, and he's hit. Pop cannot make it down the hatch; but nevertheless, he gives the order to "Take her down!" Duke tries to save him but it's either the lives of 80 men, or Pop. The sub crash-dives, leaving the dying skipper in the sea. On the command of Duke (now skipper) the *Thunderfish* dives under the freighter and comes up fighting. She rams the freighter, sinking her. But the sub is heavily damaged.

The sub manages to get back to Pearl, where Duke is summoned before a routine Navy board of inquiry. The board recommends that Duke be sent back to the States for a rest.

Duke sees the admiral in charge of submarine operations and asks to be assigned to the *Thunderfish*. But he must settle for a stay at Pearl Harbor conducting experiments on the faulty torpedoes. Duke and the special group assigned to him solve the problem and Duke gets his ship back. The *Thunderfish* intercepts the battle line of the Imperial Fleet near Leyte in the Philippines and alerts Pearl Harbor, which notifies the American Third and Seventh fleets. The *Thunderfish* rescues downed flyers and heads back to Pearl victorious.

Leo E. Kuter, who designed the sets for two previous submarine pictures, *Destination Tokyo* and

Operation Pacific includes background shots which were taken at what is now Camp H.M. Smith and a Honolulu police station. In this scene, John Wayne and his crew are jailed after a wild night on the town in Honolulu. Superstar Wayne made many Hawai'i- and Pacific-related films.

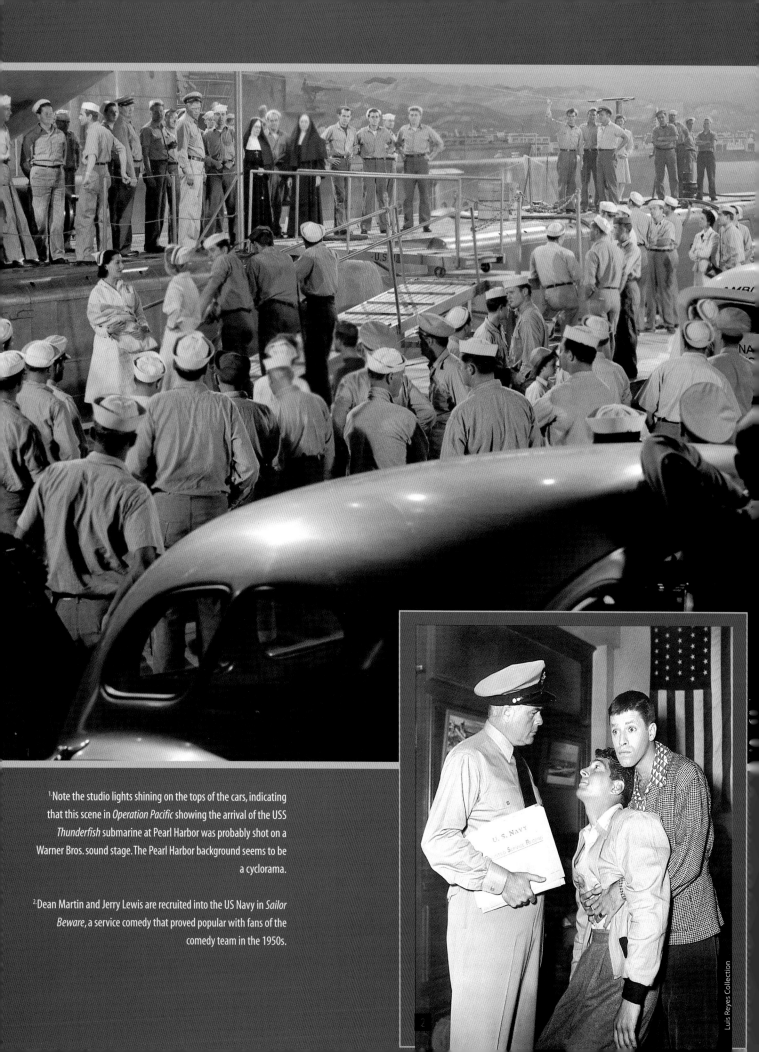

[1] Note the studio lights shining on the tops of the cars, indicating that this scene in *Operation Pacific* showing the arrival of the USS *Thunderfish* submarine at Pearl Harbor was probably shot on a Warner Bros. sound stage. The Pearl Harbor background seems to be a cyclorama.

[2] Dean Martin and Jerry Lewis are recruited into the US Navy in *Sailor Beware*, a service comedy that proved popular with fans of the comedy team in the 1950s.

Northern Pursuit, also served as art director on *Operation Pacific.* His highly technical and detailed knowledge of submarines made the sets authentic in every detail from periscope to diving plates. The sets included the interior of a conning tower, the control and radio room, the crew's mess and galley, the officers' wardroom and forward torpedo room, as well as the exterior of an entire submarine. A giant replica of a submarine was constructed on a mammoth water tank studio sound stage, geared to hold 623,000 gallons of water. John Wayne and Patricia Neal would be reunited at Pearl Harbor 15 years later in similar roles in Otto Preminger's *In Harm's Way.*

SAILOR BEWARE

Paramount Pictures, 1951

D: Hal Walker

S: James Allardice, Martin Rackin, Elwood Ullmar, John Grant

P: Hal B. Wallis

Cast: Dean Martin, Jerry Lewis, Corine Calvet

This was the fifth comedy in three years for the team of Martin and Lewis. In 1951, they were voted the #2 box-office attraction by U.S. theatrical film exhibitors. The film follows the boys through the rigors of boot camp. After training is completed, the Navy decides to send them to Hawai'i. They perform their funny routines against the background of a training base in Hawai'i and a submarine. Location scenes were filmed at the San Diego Naval Training Station. This movie marked the first big-screen appearance of legendary actor James Dean (*Rebel Without a Cause, Giant*) in a small role as a Navy man in Hawai'i. Look for him in a locker room set in Honolulu during the film's boxing sequence.

BIG JIM MCLAIN

Warner Bros. 1952

D: Edward Ludwig

S: James Edward Grant

P: Wayne/Fellows Productions

Cast: John Wayne, Nancy Olson, James Arness

This was one of the first postwar motion pictures to be filmed substantially in Hawai'i and, as such, it becomes a filmed record of then-contemporary Hawai'i. When they first arrive in Honolulu to investigate Communist activities in the island territory, McLain (Wayne) and his partner (Arness) make a brief visit to the site of the fallen *Arizona* at Pearl Harbor and drop two flower leis in memoriam.

John Wayne and James Arness take time out from their duties routing communists in postwar Hawai'i in *Big Jim McLain* to honor the fallen heroes at the site of the USS *Arizona* in Pearl Harbor. The routine, lackluster movie was filmed entirely on location in Hawai'i and featured many locals and many scenic, well-known landmarks.

1. Location shooting aboard a Naval ship with Tom Tully and Humphrey Bogart in the World War II court-martial drama *The Caine Mutiny*. Bogart was rarely better as the demented Captain Queeg; nobody can ever forget the nervous rolling of those metal balls around in his hand when he sat in the witness stand!

2. Van Johnson in a scene from *The Caine Mutiny*.

THE CAINE MUTINY

Columbia Pictures, 1954

D: Edward Dmytryk

S: Stanley Roberts, from the novel by Herman Wouk

P: Stanley Kramer

Cast: Humphrey Bogart, Fred MacMurray, Jose Ferrer, Van Johnson

This court-martial drama of a mutiny against a psychotic captain aboard the USS *Caine*, a minesweeper during World War II, was based on the 1951 best-selling Pulitzer Prize-winning novel by Herman Wouk (who later wrote *The Winds of War* and *War and Remembrance*). Much of the action takes place in and around Pearl Harbor and the Pacific theater of war in 1944.

For the record, no mutiny has ever occurred aboard a United States Naval ship. Filmed on location at Pearl Harbor, San Francisco and Yosemite National Park.

(Left to right) Fred MacMurray, Robert Francis, Van Johnson and Humphrey Bogart in The Caine Mutiny.

THE COURT MARTIAL OF BILLY MITCHELL

Warner Bros., 1955

D: Otto Preminger

S: Milton Sperling and Emmet Lavery

P: Milton Sperling

Cast: Gary Cooper, Ralph Bellamy, Rod Steiger, Elizabeth Montgomery, Jack Lord, Peter Graves

A talky, static courtroom drama based on the true story of Brigadier General William Mitchell (1879-1936), played by Gary Cooper, who championed the viability of a strong air force. In 1921, he demonstrated how an airplane loaded with bombs could sink a battleship to prove to his superiors the value of air power.

The year was 1925 and, in light of the airplane's effective use in World War I, Mitchell accused the Army and Navy of criminal negligence for their failure to begin developing an air force. In 1925 a rash of fatal aviation accidents in both the Army and Navy due to operation of obsolete and unsafe equipment led to the crash and death of Mitchell's personal friend, Zach Landsdowne.

He accepted a court-martial as the only way to publicize the Army's neglect of air power. This military trial captured the attention of the press and, consequently, the American public. During the trial, while articulating the short-sightedness of the non-flying Army generals and the inadequacy of the aerial force, Mitchell made the shocking prediction that Japan would eventually attack the American possessions of Hawai'i and the Philippines with carrier-launched air raids without a declaration of war, and that the Army Air Corps would be unable to defend itself against these raids.

One of the men sitting in on the court-martial was then-Major General Douglas MacArthur, who 16 years later would have to deal firsthand with the Japanese sneak attack Mitchell had so accurately predicted.

In 1946, President Truman posthumously awarded a Congressional Medal of Honor to Billy Mitchell, as a way to both honor him and formally apologize for the military's grave error.

In the strong cast were a number of then-unknowns, including three who would go on to become the stars of hit TV series in the 1960s and 70s: Elizabeth Montgomery (in her film debut), would later star as Samantha on *Bewitched*, Jack Lord became McGarrett on the long running *Hawaii Five-0*, and Richard Daly found fame on *Medical Center*.

AWAY ALL BOATS

Universal, 1956

D: Joseph Pevney

S: Ted Sherdiman, based on an original story by Kevin Dodson

P: Howard Christie

Cast: Jeff Chandler, George Nader, Lex Barker, Richard Boone, Julie Adams, John McIntire, Lee Marvin, Claude Akins

This is the story of Naval amphibious operations in the Pacific from Makin Island to Okinawa during World War II. In late 1943, Pearl Harbor is history, Marines are already at Guadalcanal and the U.S. Army is in North Africa. The transport ship USS *Belinda* is an APA (Attack Personnel and Amphibious). It leaves San Francisco under the command of Guadalcanal veteran Capt. Jebediah Hawks (Chandler), and is on practice maneuvers until it reaches Pearl Harbor. Arriving at Pearl in full regalia, Hawks remarks, "That is the smartest looking ship to enter or leave Pearl Harbor." The ship's crew encounters some hurdles in its landing training on the beachheads but ultimately proves itself.

Away All Boats stars Jeff Chandler, who served in the Army during World War II. Chandler would go on to play the true-life General Frank Merrill in Samuel Fuller's *Merrill's Marauders*, which takes place in the early days of the Burma-China-India campaign of World War II. Future superstar Robert Mitchum also makes an early screen appearance here.

THE WINGS OF EAGLES

MGM, 1957

D: John Ford

S: Frank Fenton and William Wiester Haines

P: Charles Schnee

Cast: John Wayne, Maureen O'Hara, Dan Dailey, Ward Bond, Ken Curtis

This is the story of Cmdr. Frank "Spig" Wead (Wayne) and his exploits as an aviator in World War I until his retirement from the Navy at the height of World War II. Mid-career, Wead suffered an accident at home that injured his back and left his legs paralyzed. With the help of his friend, Navy mechanic Carson (Dailey), he regains the partial use of his legs. With his Naval career over, he pursues writing and finds work as a screenwriter of Navy-themed films in Hollywood. Estranged from his wife Minnie (O'Hara) for many years, Wead is at the point of a partial reconciliation when one Sunday afternoon at home there is news on the radio of the attack on Pearl Harbor. Wead goes back to active Naval duty in the Pacific and assists in the development of "jeep carriers" until a heart ailment sidelines him during combat.

Wead was a screenwriter and longtime friend of director John Ford. His last script was *They Were Expendable* (1945).

[1] Richard Boone, George Nader and Jeff Chandler on maneuvers aboard the APA USS *Belinda* in *Away All Boats*. Though it takes place in the Pacific during World War II, the movie was filmed in Puerto Rico near the island of Vieques in the Caribbean, where Marine and Naval maneuvers were filmed before the Technicolor widescreen cameras.

[2] John Wayne embraces Maureen O'Hara as their faithful friend Dan Daily watches their squadron during flying exercises in *The Wings of Eagles*, the true story of naval airman and Hollywood screenwriter Frank "Spig" Wead.

TORPEDO RUN

MGM, 1958

D: Joseph Pevney

S: Richard Sale and William Wister Haines

P: Edmund Grainger

Cast: Glenn Ford, Ernest Borgnine, Dean Jones, Diane Brewster, Paul Picerni

This story is set in the South Pacific, 10 months after the attack on Pearl Harbor. The Japanese aircraft carrier *Shinaru* is the U.S. Navy's number-one target since it led the attack on Pearl Harbor.

Commander Barney Doyle (Ford) is a submarine commander worried about his wife and daughter in the Philippines whom he has not heard from since the Japanese invasion of that country. Through intelligence reports he hears that they are alive and being held in a Japanese prison camp. Some time later, he is instructed to go after the *Shinaru*, but he soon learns that it is being screened by a transport ship that is carrying prisoners of war—including his wife and daughter. When Doyle's sub encounters the aircraft carrier, he orders a torpedo attack, but tragically the carrier is untouched while the transport ship is hit and sunk, killing all on board. Haunted by this fact, he pursues the *Shinaru* into Tokyo Bay and sinks her.

Ernest Borgnine tries to liven up his sullen captain Glenn Ford, in Torpedo Run.

A flashback scene takes place in the Philippines at a birthday celebration at home for his daughter. Barney, out of love and concern, says to his wife, "You know what's coming. You know what can happen here." His wife remarks that she was born and raised in Manila and if there is trouble she will hide in the hills with their daughter until Barney gets back. A servant interrupts the party with the announcement that there is a call for Commander Doyle: "The Naval base is excited; something about Pearl Harbor." Other scenes take place at Pearl Harbor with the commander of submarine Pacific fleet and its communication center.

Scenes in the Philippines were shot in Santa Monica and the Palos Verde Peninsula, and the Pearl Harbor scenes at the MGM studios.

RUN SILENT, RUN DEEP

United Artists, 1958

D: Robert Wise

S: John Gay

P: Harold Hecht

Cast: Clark Gable, Burt Lancaster, Jack Warden, Brad Dexter, Don Rickles

The scenes set at Pearl Harbor in this WWII submarine action film were filmed at Palos Verde Peninsula near Los Angeles and studio military office interiors at a Hollywood sound stage. This is a taut action film about underwater warfare in the Pacific theatre, and highly recommended. Note the future king of comedic insults, Don Rickles, in a rare dramatic role as a submariner.

UP PERISCOPE

Warner Bros. 1959

D: Gordon Douglas

S: Robert Landau, from the novel by Robb White

P: Aubrey Schenck

Cast: James Garner, Edmond O'Brien, Alan Hale Jr.

Somewhere in the Pacific in 1942, Paul Stevenson (O'Brien) is a by-the-book submarine commander whose strict handling of situations leads to the eventual death of a seriously wounded

1 Ernest Borgnine and Glenn Ford star as officers in a World War II submarine story of the relentless chase of a Japanese aircraft carrier following the attack on Pearl Harbor. Ford is the commanding officer with a supporting role played by Borgnine as one of the junior officers in *Torpedo Run*.

2 Ernest Borgnine, Paul Picerni, Dean Jones and Glenn Ford in *Torpedo Run*.

James Garner and Alan Hale appearing in a scene from the Warner Bros. production of *Up Periscope*. The versatile Garner worked in both feature films and television but found his niche as television's *Maverick* and later Jim Rockford on *The Rockford Files*. Alan Hale became most identified as the befuddled Skipper on the TV comedy *Gilligan's Island*.

man. Lt. Braden (Garner) is an underwater demolition expert recruited by Naval Intelligence in San Diego. He is flown to Pearl Harbor and given a top-secret mission. He is to gather information at an enemy-held island communication center in order to decipher a code. Commander Stevenson's submarine is ordered to transport Braden but Stevenson's strict military tactics threaten the success of the mission. The island is believed to be Kosrae, now part of the Federated States of Micronesia.

James Garner, a Warner Bros. contract player at the time of this film, would become a major film and television star as a result of his starring role on the popular Warner Bros. television series *Maverick*. His film credits include *The Americanization Of Emily*, *Support Your Local Sheriff* and *Victor Victoria*. In the late seventies he also starred in the hit television series *The Rockford Files*. Alan Hale Jr., the son of the famous character actor, followed in his father's footsteps until the role of the Skipper on *Gilligan's Island* made him a television favorite.

HELL TO ETERNITY

Allied Artists, 1960

D: Phil Karlson

S: Ted Sherdeman and Walter Roeber Schmidt, based on a story by Gail Doud

P: Irving H. Levin

Cast: Jeffrey Hunter, David Janssen, Vic Damone, Sessue Hayakawa, George Takei

This is the true story of U.S. Marine war hero Guy Gabaldon (Hunter), a Mexican-American orphan from East Los Angeles who was adopted by a Japanese-American family prior to World War II. His knowledge of the Japanese language and culture, coupled with his fighting ability, constituted a huge asset during the crucial battle of Saipan in the Pacific theater of war. Gabaldon faced a crisis of conscience when his Japanese-American family was forcibly interned in a stateside prison camp during the war. In Saipan he took hundreds of Japanese prisoners and managed to use his Japanese-language capabilities to reduce the loss of life in the process.

As a young man, Gabaldon takes his brother's girlfriend out to a drive-in restaurant where the radio is blasting some important news. A racial slur towards Japanese directed at Guy and the girl ends in a fistfight. At the moment that the fight is broken up the radio can be clearly heard to say that the Japanese have attacked Pearl Harbor and Guy realizes what has taken place.

The following scene has the family huddled around the radio listening to Roosevelt's address to Congress and the declaration of war. Guy and his two younger brothers decide to enlist when Kaz, the older brother, says when he tried to enlist he was laughed at and treated as though he was the enemy. Gabaldon reacts bitterly, "if they won't take my brothers, then the hell with them!"

Due to Executive Order 9066, Japanese-Americans are forcibly removed from their homes and placed in internment camps. Gabaldon, saddened, reflects that "they don't put German-Americans or Italian-Americans in camps."

After the family is interned, two of the brothers join the all-Nisei 442nd Regiment that fought in Italy and Germany.

In the film, tall and handsome actor Jeffrey Hunter (*The Searchers*, *King Of Kings*) plays the lead role. In contrast, the real Gabaldon was originally turned down for military service because of his age and diminutive size.

This was the first postwar dramatic feature film to sensitively feature the stateside internment of Japanese-Americans during the war.

Sessue Hayakawa, who plays the Japanese general, had been a major star of silent cinema and was at this time enjoying a resurgence in popularity after his role (again as a Japanese general) in the international hit film directed by David Lean, *Bridge On the River Kwai*.

David Janssen would go on to find major television success starring in the long-running series *The Fugitive*. George Takei, who plays George (one of the brothers), would find enduring fame as Sulu on the original *Star Trek* TV series and later theatrical movies. Vic Damone was a very popular singer of the time who did not make a successful move into acting though he was very good here. The movie was filmed on location at Camp Pendleton, Hollywood, and Okinawa.

THE GALLANT HOURS

United Artists, 1960

D: Robert Montgomery

S: Beirne Lay, Jr., Frank D. Gilroy

P: A Cagney-Montgomery Production

C: James Cagney, Dennis Weaver, James T. Goto, James Yaga

This biopic about Admiral William H. "Bull" Halsey stars Jimmy Cagney as Imperial Tokyo's public enemy number one. The film begins and ends with a solemn shipside ceremony on November 22, 1945. Halsey reminisces with his Filipino manservant about his career, and the film flashes back to the Annapolis Naval Academy, where Halsey was a cadet in 1904. The black-and-white feature follows Halsey through the Naval battles in the Pacific theatre and reveals him to be a man with the common touch and who is a somewhat quirky

man—although brave in battle, Halsey's afraid of needles. A running gag in the film is Halsey's avoiding doctors and shots. *The Gallant Hours* ends with the post-VJ-Day ceremony aboard ship, wherein the Admiral relinquishes his command, now that the war—with his help—has been won.

The film includes several references to Pearl Harbor, particularly in relation to the architect of that attack, the commander of the Japanese Navy. Probably the most interesting thing about this biopic is that throughout the film, Admiral Halsey is counterpointed with his Imperial counterpart—Admiral Yamamoto, who also graduated from a Naval Academy, class of '04. Once again, Yamamoto is portrayed as a tragic Shakespearean character, torn between certainty that Japan's fighting a lost cause and his loyalty to Hirohito and country.

The most gripping aspect of *The Gallant Hours* is the showdown between Yamamoto and Halsey. A Japanese message regarding Yamamoto's top secret flight plans is sent to decoders in Washington and, ironically, Pearl. When the Admiral flies to Bougainville in 1943, U.S. Army P-38s shoot down his plane, killing Halsey's nemesis. *The Gallant Hours* makes a fine companion film to Toshiro Mifune's *Admiral Yamamoto*.

However, *The Gallant Hours* could've been called "The Gabby Hours and Hours"—it is probably the talkiest war film in motion picture history. Somehow, as the film gallivants across the Pacific and through warfare at Guadalcanal, nary a single solitary battle is shown. The recurring hymnal music as well as the narration are too elegiac in tone. Halsey is never called by his nickname "Bull," and there's too much reverence for a plainspoken, sometimes irreverent, if indeed great, man. Perhaps this is because Cagney produced and released this film through United Artists with his brother William (as they also did with the far livelier *Blood on the Sun*). Director Robert Montgomery was a WWII veteran who co-starred with John Wayne in the Philippines-set wartime drama *They Were Expendable* (which Montgomery reportedly co-directed with John Ford). Montgomery's daughter, Elizabeth, went on to star in the *Bewitched* TV series; *The Gallant Hours* could've used a twitch of Samantha's nose for an infusion of movie magic—or Cagney smashing a grapefruit in Yamamoto's face (as he had done to Mae Clark in a famous scene in 1931's *Public Enemy*, Cagney's breakthrough picture).

WACKIEST SHIP IN THE ARMY

Columbia Pictures, 1961

D: Richard Murphy

S: Richard Murphy; adaptation by Herbert Margolis and William Raynor, based on a story by Herbert Carlson

P: Fred Kohlmar

Cast: Jack Lemmon, Ricky Nelson, John Lund, Chips Rafferty, Tom Tully

Lt. Rip Crandall (Lemmon), a peacetime yachtsman, joins the Navy during World War II and is given a schooner to skipper. Much to his consternation, he has to teach the crew members about the operation of a sailing ship. Disguised as a native trading craft, the vessel and its crew are sent on a secret mission to a Japanese-held island. The idea for the film came from an actual wartime mission on a sailing vessel under orders from Army Gen. Douglas MacArthur in 1943, which explains the title.

Filmed mostly on location on Kaua'i, the company then moved to Pearl Harbor for some location scenes, to find the harbor full of the necessary Navy craft. The fleet, which had been there the entire time the company was on Kauai, had sailed out the night before they arrived in Pearl Harbor.

UNDER SIEGE

Warner Bros., 1992

D: Andrew Davis

S: J.F. Lawton

P: Arnon Milchan, Steven Seagal, Steven Reuther

Cast: Steven Seagal, Tommy Lee Jones, Gary Busey

The battleship USS *Missouri* is being decommissioned by President Bush in Hawai'i. (Actual news footage is integrated into the opening of the movie.) The USS *Missouri* welcomes aboard the musicians and caterers set to provide entertainment during the famed battleship's last voyage. But two of these visitors unexpectedly throw their own party, since they're actually a rogue CIA operative (Jones) and a turncoat naval officer (Busey). These killer elite commandos hijack the ship's nuclear armaments and threaten to blow up Honolulu. They overpower the crew—except for one man. He's chief cook Casey Ryback (Seagal), an ex-Navy Seal and highly decorated combat operative. Relying on martial-arts skills and advanced weaponry, Ryback turns the ship into a combat zone.

Though it is set on the USS *Missouri*, principal filming took place on the USS *Alabama*, which is drydocked in (appropriately) Alabama.

CRIMSON TIDE

Buena Vista, 1995

D: Tony Scott

S: Michael Schiffer and Richard P. Henrick

P: Jerry Bruckheimer and Don Simpson

Cast: Denzel Washington, Gene Hackman, George Dzunda, Matt Craven

When radio communication problems aboard the USS *Alabama* (a submarine with nuclear strike capability) prevent the ship from receiving orders clearly during a tense confrontation with a Russian warship, Naval Officer Hunter (Washington) faces a huge ethical dilemma. Does he countermand the orders of veteran Naval commander Captain Ramsey (Hackman) to fire nuclear missiles, or follow his command and risk launching an unprovoked nuclear war?

The last scenes of the film take place at U.S. Naval headquarters at Pearl Harbor, where the two commanders go before an Admiral's board of inquiry to reach an understanding and then go on with their lives.

1. Trapped on the USS *Missouri* at
sea, Ryback (Steven Seagal, center)
talks to the Pentagon as his
crew— Ramirez (Raymond Cruz),
Granger (Troy Evans), Jordan (Erika
Eleniak) and Tackman (Damian
Chapa)—listen in the action
thriller *Under Siege*.

2. Left to right: Ricky Nelson and Jack
Lemmon on Kaua'i location for
Wackiest Ship in the Army.

Gene Hackman and Denzel Washington co-star in *Crimson Tide,* whose final scenes take place at Pearl Harbor Naval headquarters. The final scene also employs the late respected American stage and screen actor Jason Robards as an Admiral in the court of inquiry scene. Robards was featured as Lt. General Walter C. Short in *Tora! Tora! Tora!* Robards was a radio operator in the United States Navy on the morning of December 7, 1941 and witnessed the attack on "Battleship Row" from his ship, the USS *Honolulu,* across Pearl Harbor's south channel.

CHAPTER 5
Pearl Harbor on Television

PEARL HARBOR ON TELEVISION

THE ATTACK ON Pearl Harbor was an immediate radio event. In the years immediately after the war, television began to give it further legendary status. Succeeding generations were exposed to newsreel footage of that day of infamy in a continuing barrage of news reports and documentaries airing on local and network television spanning over five decades. Some of the most memorable programs were NBC's Emmy award-winning *Victory At Sea* (1952), CBS's *The Twentieth Century* (1957-1970), and ABC's U.S. Army-sponsored *The Big Picture* (1953-1959).

Newsreel images of the smoking *Arizona's* crumpled structure, the panning shot of the wreckage of the ships in the harbor, the clock on the Aloha Tower, Diamond Head, a stilled Waikīkī and a neighborhood in flames have been rerun thousands of times in our collective memory.

Many World War II-era movies made their way to television to form a staple of programming through the fifties and sixties. Before afternoon talk shows and reality programming filled the airwaves, kids would still watch old black-and-white movies, since color televisions were still a big-ticket item. And a growing awareness of civil rights and the offensiveness of ethnic stereotypes hadn't yet pushed off the air the negative depictions of Asians, African-Americans or Native Americans sometimes found in these films.

Even with the hundreds of thousands of hours of television produced by the American television networks, there has been very little dramatic programming produced on Pearl Harbor.

The first dramatic series with a Pearl Harbor connection was the 1958 Westinghouse Desilu Playhouse pilot episode for the series that developed into Rod Serling's *The Twilight Zone*.

The Hawaii-set detective series *Hawaiian Eye* (1959-1963) featured shots of contemporary Pearl Harbor, and one episode, "The Second Day Of Infamy," dealt with a former Japanese saboteur who escapes from a mental hospital thinking it is the eve of December 7, 1941.

Hawaii Five-O (1968-1980) was the first television series filmed completely on location in Hawai'i. Steve McGarrett was a Naval reserve officer as well as being the head of the Five-O crime fighting unit. Many episodes took place in and around Pearl Harbor and other island military facilities, as well as aboard U.S. Navy and Coast Guard ships. One episode, "To Hell With Babe Ruth," shared many plot similarities with *Hawaiian Eye's* "The Second Day Of Infamy."

Magnum P.I. (1980-1988), another long-running Hawai'i-filmed series, was about a private detective who was a former Naval officer. It too utilized Pearl Harbor as a background for contemporary story locations.

The advent of the television miniseries exemplified by *Roots* (1977), where a large audience could be held for several nights with a spectacular presentation of a celebrated novel, became the perfect format for the first Hawai'i-set miniseries *Pearl* (1978). This was a five-hour adaptation by Stirling Silliphant of a script he would turn into a novel to appear with the airing of the program. This was followed by a similar adaptation of James Jones' *From Here To Eternity* (1979) and a short-lived series. The 1983 Herman

The cast of *McHale's Navy*—on top in the straw hat and aloha shirt is Ernest Borgnine (who also co-starred in 1953's WWII drama *From Here to Eternity*) as the PT boat commander McHale, and in uniform on the bottom is Tim Conway as Ensign Parker.

Luis Reyes Collection

Wouk 18-hour miniseries *The Winds Of War* (starring Robert Mitchum) featured a Pearl Harbor attack, but it was filmed at Port Hueneme, California. The 36-hour miniseries *War and Remembrance* (1988) filmed portions on Oʻahu and Pearl Harbor, re-creating Naval engagements of the Pacific theater of World War II.

Cable television has not developed any dramatic telefilms or series about Pearl Harbor, but it has recycled old combat, newsreel and government footage into numerous documentaries on many aspects of this period, including Pearl Harbor and Pacific battle engagements. By necessity, virtually any documentary on America's involvement in World War II has to begin with film footage of the aftermath of the attack on Pearl Harbor and Franklin Delano Roosevelt's declaration of war to Congress the following day. As opposed to television dramas, documentaries are relatively inexpensive to produce.

The release of the film *Pearl Harbor* in 2001, and the 60th anniversary of the attack, spurred creations of new Pearl Harbor-related programs on the History Channel and other little-screen venues.

SERIES

WESTINGHOUSE DESILU PLAYHOUSE

November 1958

"The Time Element"

D: Alan Reisner

T: Rod Serling

P: Bert Granet

Cast: William Bendix, Martin Balsam, Jesse White, Dwayne Hickman

This was the original pilot for the television series *The Twilight Zone*. The story takes place in then-contemporary 1958. Part-time bartender and bookie Peter Jenson (Bendix) is having a recurring dream in which he finds himself at Pearl Harbor on the eve of the attack on December 7, 1941, and no one is listening to his warnings of impending doom. He believes he is not dreaming and that somehow he is traveling through time. He tells his tale to Dr. Gillespie (Balsam), a psychiatrist who takes an interest in his dilemma. In the psychiatrist's office his dream picks up on the morning of December 7 in a Honolulu hotel room where he

hears the drone of airplane engines. He opens up the window curtains, sees Japanese planes attacking and shouts "No one listened to me!" As the planes strafe the hotel, he is killed in a hail of bullets. Back at the psychiatrist's office, Dr. Gillespie appears to have dozed off and Jenson is no longer resting on the couch. Did he really exist? Dazed, Gillespie checks his appointment book and notes that there are no appointments scheduled today. He goes to a local bar to have a drink, where he notices an old photo of Jenson, the man who walked into his office. He asks the bartender about the man in the picture. The bartender says that he used to work there many years ago but that he was killed at Pearl Harbor on Dec. 7.

Westinghouse was the sponsor of the show and did not wish to offend the U.S. Army, with which it held many contracts. So the original Rod Serling script was changed so that Jenson would not try to warn the Army of the impending attack but instead would only warn the Naval ensign, his fiancée, a bartender and some local authorities. Martin Balsam, who plays the psychiatrist, would 12 years later play Admiral Kimmel in the big-budget theatrical Pearl Harbor feature film, *Tora! Tora! Tora!*.

HAWAIIAN EYE

Warner Bros.. 1959-1963

Cast: Anthony Eiseley, Robert Conrad, Connie Stevens, Poncie Ponce

Hawaiian Eye is a Honolulu-based private detective agency with its office at what is now the Hilton Hawaiian Village Hotel in Waikīkī.

Episode # 3, aired 10/21/59

#6741

"Second Day of Infamy"

D: Howard W. Koch

T: Steven Ritch

Guest Cast: Yuki Shimoda, Miiko Taka, Edward Platt

A doctor from a mental hospital asks his old friend Tracy Steele (Eiseley) to locate an escaped patient for him. It is 1959 and the patient is Mitsuki

Yato Mitsuki (Yuki Shimoda) is an escaped mental patient who, eighteen year later in 1959, believes it is the eve of Dec. 7, 1941 in the *Hawaiian Eye* episode "Second Day Of Infamy."

[1.] The cast of *Hawaiian Eye.*

[2.] James Darren, Lee Meriwether, and Robert Colbert star in the TV series *The Time Tunnel. The Time Tunnel* series turned out to be an entertaining weekly world history lesson using stock footage, costumes, props and sets from old Twentieth Century Fox historical movies. James Darren was a popular teen idol and singer of the late fifties who became an accomplished actor. His film credits range from *Gidget* to *The Guns Of Navarone.* Lee Meriwether was a former Miss America.

(Shimoda), a former Japanese saboteur who landed in the Islands a few months before Pearl Harbor. Captured on December 7 with a head wound which affected his memory, he has remained in the hospital ever since. One day he has a relapse and believes it is December 1941, a few days before the Pearl Harbor attack. He escapes to present-day Pearl Harbor and sees no fleet there. He wants to warn the Imperial Navy that the fleet is gone from Pearl Harbor and to complete his mission of dynamiting a fuel depot. Steele and his partner Tom Lopaka's (Conrad) only clue to finding him is a former Japanese nightclub dancer, Sumiko (Taka) whom the patient was acquainted with 18 years previously. Mitsuki goes to the home of Sumiko, now married and the mother of a child. He threatens her if she doesn't help him. Steele, with Lopaka's help, has found out where Sumiko lives, and comes to the house to ask if she's seen Mitsuki. After a wild chase, Tracy finds Mitsuki about to blow up a fuel depot. Police arrive in time to prevent the explosion.

The script idea for this episode was later recycled to service another Hawai'i-based crime series almost ten years later on *Hawaii Five-O* as the episode "To Hell With Babe Ruth." *Hawaiian Eye* used Asian-American actors Yuki Shimoda (*A Majority Of One*) and Miiko Taka (*Sayonara*) in the leading guest roles, as opposed to the *Hawaii Five-O* episode which used Caucasian actors playing Asians with the aid of makeup and prosthetics. In an interesting quote from the *Hawaiian Eye* script, Mitsuki states to Sumiko: "The Japanese in Hawai'i can't be trusted because they are Americans first, Hawaiian second and then Japanese."

THE TIME TUNNEL

1966-1967

Irwin Allen created and produced this one-hour series about a secret tunnel-like device in a laboratory under the auspices of the U.S. government that gives two scientists the ability to travel in time and space.

Episode #4
"The Day the Sky Fell Down"
T: Ellis St. John
D: William Hale
Cast: James Darren, Robert Colbert, Lee
    Meriwether
Guest Cast: Linden Chiles, Sam Groom, Lew
    Gallo, Caroline Kido, Susan
    Flannery

In the same manner as each episode of this series began, Tony (Darren) and Doug (Colbert) suddenly materialize in the Japanese consulate in Honolulu on the day before the attack on Pearl Harbor. They are able to talk their way out of the consulate. They try to warn Tony's father, a Naval officer who was reported missing after the attack. Tony meets himself as a 7-year old boy and sees how his father died. The Pearl Harbor attack sequence was constructed from stock color footage from Ford's *December 7th*. Darren's two previous Hawai'i-related feature film roles were in *Gidget Goes Hawaiian* (1961) and *Diamond Head* (1962). This time, however, he did not get to enjoy any on-location filming.

TIC-TOC

HAWAII FIVE-0

CBS, 1968-1980

Cast: Jack Lord, James MacArthur, Kam Fong, Zulu, Herman Wedemeyer, Richard Denning

A crime series set in the lush surroundings of Hawai'i. Hawaii Five-0 was the longest-running drama series in TV history. Its telescript writers included former Hunter College, New York screenwriting professor Jerome Coopersmith (who first visited Hawai'i five years after he started writing Five-0) and Samoan screenwriter Johnny Knuebuhl. The plot centers on a four-man Hawai'i state police unit headed by Steve McGarrett (Lord), who, according to the script, reported only to the governor.

McGarrett gives frequent service to Naval Intelligence at Pearl Harbor, both as the head of Five-0 and as a commander in the Navy Reserve (although Lord reportedly served in the Merchant Marines during WWII.). In a Dec. 11, 1979 interview with *Daily Variety*, Jack Lord praised "the exceptional cooperation of the U.S. Navy. In fact, all of the services, the Coast Guard, Army and Air Force have been more than generous with their help, advice and facilities." Emerging during the Vietnam War era, *Five-0* reflected Cold War propaganda of the period. About 10% of the scripts had anti-communist themes, including leftist terrorist groups, although Hawai'i-based intelligence sources report that there was no such activity then. McGarrett's nemesis, Wo Fat (Khiegh Dhiegh) was a Chinese Communist agent of Chairman Mao. *Five-0* perpetuated the anti-communism of 1952's *Big Jim McLain*, and top cop McGarrett's name seems inspired by John Wayne's character. In 1962's *Dr. No*, Lord joined Sean Connery as the ultimate espionage cold warrior, James Bond. Lord plays 007's cohort, CIA agent Felix Leiter, in the anti-Chinese spy flick that triggered the most successful movie franchise in history, the Bond pictures.

Season 2
Episode # 25
"To Hell With Babe Ruth"
written by Anthony Lawrence, directed by Nicholas Colasanto

Cast: Jack Lord, , Kam Fong, James MacArthur, Zulu

Guest Cast: Mark Lenard, Will Kuluva, Virginia Wing

A Japanese saboteur Yoshio Nagata (Lenard), escaping from a Honolulu mental hospital 28 years later, is determined to complete a mission from 1941. McGarrett and his team enlist the help of the military to help track down a bomb and its perpetrator. The title comes from an expression used by the Japanese pilots attacking Pearl Harbor.

The episode does make the point that no sabotage was done by any resident of Hawai'i, including the resident Japanese, during World War II.

Season 8
Episode # 169
"Murder-Eyes Only"
D: Michael O'Herlihy
T: Orville H. Hampton and Jerome Coopersmith
P: Sheldon Leonard
Cast: Jack Lord, James MacArthur, Kam Fong,
Guest Cast: Harry Guardino, David Birney, Khiegh Dhiegh
Two-hour episode

This episode features extensive views of Pearl Harbor and its environments, including the USS *Arizona*

[1.] "Book 'em, Dano!"—Jack Lord in his signature role as special unit chief Steve McGarrett in *Hawaii Five-0*.

[2.] Manu Topou, who played Prince Keoki in *Hawai'i* and later taught acting for L.A.'s American Repertory Company, is originally from Fiji. Here, he appears in an episode of the long-running TV series *Hawaii Five-0*, with Jack Lord as supercop Steve McGarrett, and France Nuyen, who also co-starred in *South Pacific* and *Diamond Head*.

Tom Selleck co-stars with Hawai'i in the title role of the long-running TV series *Magnum, P.I.*, which catapulted Selleck to fame as the lovable private eye. Despite the fact that the Aloha State has a relatively low crime rate, Hawai'i has been the setting for numerous crime movies and TV shows.

2. Royce D. Applegate as Security Chief Crocker co-stars with Roy Scheider as Captain Nathan Bridger in MCA TV International's action adventure series *SEAQUEST DSV*.

Memorial. It is filled with anti-communist hysteria, with Red China plotting against America.

MAGNUM, P.I.

CBS, 1980-1988
Cast: Tom Selleck, John Hillerman, Roger E. Mosley, Larry Manetti

Thomas Sullivan Magnum (Selleck), retired from the Navy after serving in Vietnam, turns private eye and lives an idyllic life keeping tabs on security at a lush beachfront mansion on O'ahu's windward side. His companion is the estate's knowledgeable but stuffy major-domo, Jonathan Q. Higgins (Hillerman), who disapproves intensely of Magnum's freewheeling ways. Although Magnum depicted ethnic white lead characters, an English character and an African-American, unlike its predecessor Hawaii Five-0, there are no recurring Hawaiian or local roles in this series. In real life, Selleck reportedly did not serve in Vietnam.

Season 3
Episode # 51
"Almost Home"
T: Rob Gilmer, Alan Cassidy
D: Ivan Dixon

Guest Cast: Kathleen Lloyd, Stephen Elliott, Beulah Quo

Magnum helps a young woman trying to prove her deceased father innocent of charges of desertion from Pearl Harbor on December 7, 1941, thus allowing his ashes to be buried on his ship: The USS *Arizona*.

Episode # 58
"Forty Years From Sand Island"
T: Rogers Turrentino, Rob Gilmer, Reuben Leder
D: Mike Vejar
Guest Cast: Keye Luke, James Shigeta

Higgins investigates matters relating to the Japanese internment during the war and his life is put on the line due to the secrets he is on the verge of discovering.

SEAQUEST DSV

NBC, 1993-1995
Season 2
Episode # 28
"The Sincerest Form of Flattery"
D: Jesus Salvador Trevino
Cast: Roy Scheider, Michael Ironside, Stephanie Beacham, Don Franklin, Jonathan Brandis

This was a one-hour series set in the year 2030. The flagship of the UEO (United Earth Organization) is a state-of-the-art submarine (DSV or Deep Submergence Vehicle) commanded by Captain Nathan Bridger (Scheider) on a dual mission of scientific research and military peacekeeping.

A catastrophic error in the downloading of a computerized submarine sends it on a mission of worldwide destruction beginning with the UEO Naval Base at Pearl Harbor. The submarine launches missiles at Pearl Harbor which are noticed at the tracking station there and one officer comments, "It's been

a hundred years since the Pearl Harbor sneak attack. I really don't think it's the Japanese." Another says, "I can see them; missiles. We are under attack!" The missiles strike a test-firing range, resulting in little or no damage or loss of life. The Sequest and its captain must stop the robot submarine before it causes massive death and destruction due to its nuclear armaments.

BAYWATCH, HAWAII

Syndicated 1999-2001

P: Greg Bonnan

Cast: David Hasselhoff, Jason Brooks, Brande Roderick, Michael Bergin, Stacy Kamano, Krista Allen, Jason Momoa, Charlie Brumbly

This ocean-rescue series was filmed around Hawai'i. In one episode, the grandfather of one of the lifeguards visits O'ahu, becomes distraught, and disappears. He's found crying at the USS *Utah* Memorial on Ford Island in Pearl Harbor, overcome by memories of December 7, 1941—because he was there. His granddaughter talks him out of committing suicide.

The cast of Baywatch Hawaii

Ed Rampell Collection

MINI-SERIES

PEARL

ABC, 1978-79

D: Hy Averback, Alex Singer
S: Stirling Silliphant
P: Sam Manners, Stirling Silliphant
C: Tiana Alexandra, Angie Dickinson, Dennis Weaver, Robert Wagner, Lesley Ann Warren, Adam Arkin, Brian Dennehy, Max Gail, Marion Ross, Gregg Henry, Christian Vance, Katherine Helmond, Char Fontane, Don Rockwell

"Those last three days in Pearl, there was still time for hope, still time for love," *Pearl*'s narrator says in the torrid opening sequence. This TV miniseries follows a substantial cast of characters during the hours leading up to the Battle of O'ahu, the Imperial air raid itself, and its aftermath. The lead characters are stationed at either Schofield Barracks or Pearl Harbor, and the women are their significant off-base others (and their relations), in this shot-on-location-on-O'ahu epic. Racist Colonel Jason Forrest (NBC's *McCloud*, Dennis Weaver, who'd previously played Admiral Halsey's aide in *The Gallant Hours*) and his wife Midge (NBC's *Police Woman*, Angie Dickinson) live together on-base but are estranged. Midge blames Jason's jockeying for position in the peacetime Army for negligence that led to their young daughter's death, and in that time-honored soap-opera tradition, exacts revenge via adultery.

Forrest's Executive Officer, Captain Cal Lanford (Robert Wagner, of ABC's *Hart To Hart*, which shot a 1984 episode in Hawai'i and returned to paradise a decade later for a made-for-TV movie) is a surprisingly liberal Southern gentleman. Midge fails to seduce Cal in his swimming pool, and he then falls for Carol (Lesley Ann Warren), a troubled, suicidal doctor wracked with guilt over her husband's death. The Finger (Christian Vance), a pretty-boy infantryman accused of homosexuality, is transferred out of his unit to serve as the chauffeur of Colonel Forrest. (Midge succeeds in seducing him in a sugar cane field.) Dogface John Zawalsky (Adam Arkin of CBS' *Chicago Hope*) is the Finger's buddy, as well as a temperamental painter, who has a relationship with Shirley (Char Fontane), a hooker.

The cast of the TV series *Baywatch Hawaii* starring David Hasselhoff during its first season. *Baywatch* was the most popular show in syndication history for ten years and relocated to Hawai'i, under the name *Baywatch Hawaii*, for two more seasons.

Born and raised on Oʻahu, Doug North (Gregg Henry) is a haole military brat, coerced by family tradition into joining the service. But the Naval Lt. J.G. is planning to resign his commission when he is smitten by former Lincoln High schoolmate Holly Nagata (Tiana Alexandra), an AJA reporter for a Honolulu daily who has (in the parlance of the 1940s) "moxie." Screened in three two-hour segments, there are more subplots in *Pearl* than pages in this book, but the most interesting one revolves around Holly.

On assignment, Holly covers Colonel Forrest's speech, which espouses racist views about the inferiority of hapa children and a supposed Japanese conspiracy to populate, and hence take over, Oʻahu. At this haoles-only function in the Royal Hawaiian, the spirited minority journalist questions and challenges the white supremacist. Holly debunks his specious theories and walks out on him. The American-born daughter of immigrant parents schooled in the old country, Holly respects her mother and father, but they nonetheless reject her affair with the non-Japanese Naval officer. Alone in his car, parked near a beach, the forward, audacious beauty asks the shy Doug to make love with her.

That night—December 6, 1941—when Carol starts to make love with Cal, she experiences an anxiety attack, and decides to leave Hawaiʻi. (Coitus interruptus is a recurring theme in Pearl pix—before a conflicted Rafe ships out to join the RAF and fight the Battle of Britain in *Pearl Harbor*, he panics and fails to have sex with his nurse girlfriend, Evelyn.) The following morning, during a gala ship departure at Honolulu Harbor, the guilt-filled Carol tells Cal that her former husband joined the RAF and was killed during the Battle of Britain. (In *Pearl Harbor* Evelyn believes Rafe is killed—in the RAF, during—you guessed it—the Battle of Britain. Another plot similarity is that both stories are not completely true.) Carol is prevented from leaving Hawaiʻi on a passenger ship by Zeros zooming over iconic Aloha Tower, as the Battle of Oʻahu begins.

In the early morning, Doug and Holly go to the Byodo-In Temple at the Valley of the Temples. (In reality, this replica of a famous Japanese structure wasn't built until the 1960s.) There she lights incense near a huge Buddha statue, and they hear planes…Later, at a beach, they hear bombs, and their car radio announces Oʻahu is under attack. Although Doug had intended to leave the military, he patriotically rushes back to Pearl Harbor to defend Hawaiʻi, driven by the fearless Holly.

A bomb blows Doug out of the launch transporting him, and the Naval Lt. swims through flaming oil-slicked water to board a battleship, which a lifesaver identifies as the USS *Arizona*. Cut to the Japanese command center, which says the *Arizona* is already sunk, and a second wave is launched. Doug mans a machine gun, which jams, and he is blown off of the doomed *Arizona* (which contrary to the film's assertion has not sunk yet).

At the Nagata home, Holly's brother Danny (Mike Miyashiro) goes ballistic during the attack, screaming at his issei parents "Never speak Japanese to me again!" as he symbolically smashes household cultural artifacts, such as a samurai helmet, with a baseball bat. As if he is fulfilling a previously hatched state-of-siege scheme, outside the downtown Honolulu office of the *Hawaii Times*, Colonel Forrest announces: "We're taking over," as martial law is imposed. FBI agents, fearful that the father's pigeons may carry messages to enemy subs, visit the Nagatas. In impotent rage, Mr. Nagata (Seth Sakai) kills all of his cherished birds in their coop, in front of the G-men. Locals run into the streets with their belongings as Zeros soar over Honolulu.

Danny joins his ROTC comrades—AJAs—and goes to a beachhead, where they volunteer to help fight possible Japanese invaders. Holly goes to the hospital where she helps the wounded with Carol, who has rallied her spirits to help save lives (similarly, nurse Evelyn does the same in the screen's 2001 incarnation of the Pearl story). The madame of a Hotel Street brothel, Sally (Katherine Helmond), leads her hookers to the hospital to give blood to the wounded. A male doctor declines their services, but they're assigned the tasks of collecting Coke bottles for hospital use.

Colonel Forrest seizes ʻIolani Palace, apparently staging a preplanned military *coup d'etat* that ousts the civilian territorial government which was then headquartered there. A wounded Doug is wheeled into the hospital, as part two of the miniseries fades out.

In *Pearl*'s grand finale, cabbie Moe Keale drives Midge all around Oʻahu during the blitz, and calls her "one crazy haole!" Sally tells Midge: "The world is dying all around us this morning. Aloha, my Hawaiʻi." Holly sees Doug in the hospital. The stricken Lieutenant tells Holly, "my parents will love you," and proposes from his hospital bed. Holly accepts. Elsewhere on Oʻahu, Sgt. Cheney—who caught Midge in the act with the Finger and tried to blacklist her—calls Midge "the Colonel's slut."

The Finger tries to fight the sergeant, and goes on to crash Forrest's car. Zawalsky unsuccessfully tries to rescue his friend, but the Finger dies. When the Colonel is informed of the accident, he calls the Finger "that homo!" and only expresses concern for his burnt car.

An AJA courier on motorcycle tries to deliver an RCA telegram for the commanding general at Fort Shafter. The message from General George C. Marshall in Washington warning of a Japanese attack was received at 7:33 a.m., but because the cable was not marked "urgent," it is only being delivered now—too late to be of any use. The messenger is stopped at an Army roadblock in the O'ahu countryside. At the beach fortifications, a sergeant played by Max Gail (from TV's *Barney Miller*) ponders a possible third attack wave or invasion. The ammo belts for his machine guns date from WWI, and are too antiquated to be useful.

At the hospital, Carol tells Holly that Doug has died, and the reporter once so full of chutzpah finally breaks down. Holly goes to the Royal Hawaiian, where Doug's visiting parents are staying. The Norths tearfully embrace the AJA fiancée; Mrs. North (Marion Ross of TV's *Happy Days*) hugs her as they weep in one another's arms.

U.S. soldiers round up Buddhist monks. Colonel Forrest—who has missed all of the combat—issues edicts from the Palace, including the chaining of all O'ahu dogs so they won't bite his troops. Captain Lanford can't bear his C.O. anymore and requests a transfer to combat duty. Forrest refuses, and tells Cal how much he hates the Southerner because he was born into money, while Forrest is a son of the working class and has had to fight for everything he achieved. "How dare you, the rich ruling class, defend minorities?" he asks.

Out at sea, aboard a Japanese cruiser, Imperial combatants are angry that a third strike is not ordered. An Admiral laments: "At 7:55 we struck them too soon—five minutes before the declaration of war…We've lost our honor…We have mistakenly violated the international code of warfare, and in that sense we have not won a great victory. On the contrary, I'm afraid we have succeeded only in awakening a sleeping giant."

Proclaiming "Pearl Harbor—my version," Midge confronts Jason and announces she's leaving him. As curfew nears, Midge strides out of the Palace, and arranges for Carol to gain admittance, as Cal appears. She confesses to having lied about her husband, admitting that when he actually left

her, Carol created an elaborate fantasy which expressed her death wish for him. But later when he really died, Carol (who does not say how he died) was consumed with guilt. The doctor wants to stay on at the hospital—if Cal still loves her. FDR's address to Congress is heard. The deserted Colonel Forrest breaks down alone in his office. Holly goes to the Valley of the Temples. Somehow, in the four minutes left before curfew starts, Captain Lanford has managed to whisk Carol off to his beach home, with Koko Head in the distance. Pearl Harbor is seen on fire. As Aloha Tower is glimpsed (with street and clock lights on) the narrator says: "The lights of Honolulu went dark Sunday night December 7, 1941. They were to stay dark for 1,000 nights. And in that time, many others died, and many lived. But among the living, none was ever quite the same."

Pearl is largely considered to be, and is thus dismissed as, a clone of *From Here to Eternity*. Characters and plot elements seem derived from this most honored Pearl picture ever, which was based on James Jones' literary masterpiece.

But although *Pearl* is indeed greatly indebted to *Eternity*, a reconsideration shows the televised saga to be much more. Due to a combination of factors, this is one of the most interesting works in the entire Pearl pictures oeuvre. Written by Oscar winning screenwriter Sterling Silliphant, *Pearl* can be seen as a summation of the entire sub-genre of Pearl productions—all of the familiar elements are there, and then some. The miniseries format allows for extensive thematic and character development, and most importantly, the shot-on-O'ahu little-screen epic has the single most dignified local character in the entire history of Pearl pictures, which have tended to ignore Islanders.

Tiana Alexandra's spunky Holly Nagata stands out in all of the movies dealing with Pearl Harbor. Alexandra does a great job creating a three-dimensional human being with dignity and integrity, who is not a passive sex object or a victim like the AJA women interned in *Midway* and other features. In real life, Alexandra is Vietnamese; in the 1990s she created a documentary about her life called *From Hollywood to Hanoi*, and she is still active in Asian cinema.

Pearl also features other Islander characters, including the Nagatas, and a few brief Hawaiian parts. Carol's landlady is a Polynesian, and actor/musician Moe Keale (who also appeared on TV in

The Mackenzies of Paradise Cove, Big Hawaii, etc.) plays Midge's hack.

The late screenwriter Stirling Silliphant (who went on to marry Alexandra) had a history of writing minority characters and dealing with racial issues. He won an Oscar for 1967's *In the Heat of the Night* starring Sydney Poitier, and also wrote 1970's *The Liberation of L.B. Jones* and *Shaft in Africa,* as well as 1968's *Charly,* which sensitively deals with abuse of the retarded. Silliphant also wrote disaster movies such as 1974's *The Towering Inferno,* and in *Pearl,* he was able to combine his preoccupations with both racial and cataclysmic subjects.

However, writer/producer Silliphant did take some liberties with the facts in ways that are illustrative of the nature of historical fiction. The incident involving the RCA messenger with the too-late telegram from General Marshall occurred in real life much the same way as it does on screen. However, in *Pearl,* AJA motorcyclist Tadao Fuchikami is stopped at a rural O'ahu roadblock, whereas according to Lord's *Day of Infamy,* this actually took place in urban Honolulu.

A second inaccuracy is that the attack in the three-part miniseries seems as if it goes on at least all day, if not longer. Indeed, Colonel Forrest has time to move into 'Iolani Palace, and Midge to drive around O'ahu, while the bombing is underway. In point of fact, the entire air raid took slightly less than two hours. According to Lord, it began around 7:55 a.m., Hawai'i time, and ended shortly before 10:00 a.m. To serve dramatic interests, Silliphant greatly extends the time frame of the assault.

A third inaccuracy involves the Imperial Admiral and his remarks after the fighting subsided. Although Yamamoto actually expressed similar sentiments following the attack, *Pearl* doesn't mention his main regret—that U.S. carriers were not destroyed. Furthermore, Yamamoto, the mastermind of the Pearl Harbor strike, is often depicted onscreen as having been present out at sea in the task force during Operation Hawai'i. (*Pearl Harbor* repeats this factual misrepresentation.) In fact, Yamamoto was actually thousands of miles away in Japan, at Kure, in the operations room of his flagship *Nagato* (although he did communicate with the task force). While pilots such as flight leader Commander Mitsuo Fuchida did complain about the decision against continuing the offensive, movies often portray Yamamoto as giving the order not to launch another air assault against O'ahu. In fact, it was Vice Admiral

Chuichi Nagumo who did so (although this was approved the following morning by Yamamoto—who Prange assumes in *At Dawn We Slept* probably would have launched another aerial foray).

Film is an expensive mass entertainment medium, where accuracy is often sacrificed at the altar of dramatic contingencies and test screenings. It's natural in historical fiction movies for filmmakers to take creative license, to interject fictitious characters and plots into actual events. But sometimes these works are more "fiction" than "historical." Feature films can serve to whet the appetite of viewers for historic events and personalities, but in order to really learn about them, movies should be followed up with research of nonfiction sources.

FROM HERE TO ETERNITY

NBC, 1979

D: Buzz Kulik

T: Don McGuire

P: Buzz Kulik

Cast: Natalie Wood, William Devane, Peter Boyle, Roy Thinnes, Andy Griffith, Joe Pantoliano, Kim Basinger

Three-time Oscar nominee Natalie Wood, William Devane, Peter Boyle, and Andy Griffith head the all-star cast of this unabridged television version of James Jones' powerful best-seller. A six-hour miniseries about the lives of soldiers on and off duty in Hawai'i just prior to Pearl Harbor, it traces the love affair between a company commander's wife and a sergeant, and the near-brutal treatment of a young, stubborn career soldier who pays a heavy price for his principles. *From Here to Eternity* was filmed on location in Hawai'i. It was not a remake of the 1953 movie, for which only a portion of the 858-page novel was used. The contemporary miniseries format allowed for a more full and frank dramatization of the story for the first time.

Kim Basinger as Prewitt's girlfriend, the prostitute Lorene (originally played by Donna Reed in the 1953 film) in the miniseries version of *From Here to Eternity.*

FROM HERE TO ETERNITY

Series, 1979

Cast: William Devane, Barbara Hershey, Roy Thinnes, Don Johnson, Rocky Echevarria

This weekly one-hour series was drawn from the James Jones novel about Army life in Hawai'i. It was a continuance of the story originally presented in the highly successful six-hour miniseries. The locale was Honolulu, Hawai'i, six months after the Japanese attack on December 7, 1941.

In reality Jones' 25th Infantry Division fortified Makapu'u Point after the battle of Hawai'i. A plaque commemorating the *Eternity* author was erected in the mid-1990s at a ceremony attended by Kaylie Jones and other members of the James Jones Literary Society. Reverend Abraham Akaka presided over the moving Makapu'u unveiling service, honoring the writer who immortalized the Tropic Lightning Infantrymen. In 1942, the "Wolfhounds" were shipped out to Guadalcanal, and their combat exploits there were captured in Jones' *The Thin Red Line*, a sort of *Eternity* sequel filmed in the 1960s and the 1990s.

THE WINDS OF WAR

ABC, 1983

D: Dan Curtis

T: Herman Wouk

P: Dan Curtis

Cast: Robert Mitchum, Ali MacGraw, Jan-Michael Vincent, John Houseman, Peter Graves, David Dukes, Polly Bergen

This 18-hour miniseries was focused on U.S. Naval commander "Pug" Henry (Mitchum) between 1939 and the Japanese bombing of Pearl Harbor. A military attaché on a series of personal missions for President Franklin Delano Roosevelt, Pug meets all the historic titans of the period: Churchill, Hitler, Mussolini, and Stalin. He watches as the lives of his family and everyone in Europe are increasingly threatened by the gathering storm of World War II.

The bombing of Pearl Harbor was re-created at a Navy base in Port Hueneme, California, where the Navy allowed only four days of filming. Rented Navy destroyers were wired with simulated explosives. The final episode of *Winds* closes with a chickenskin reenactment of the Battle of O'ahu, one of the best ever.

BLOOD AND ORCHIDS

CBS, 1985

D: Jerry Thorpe

T: Norman Katkov

P: Andrew Adelson

Cast: Kris Kristofferson, Jane Alexander, Sean Young, Jose Ferrer, Susan Blakely, Haunani Minn, James Saito, Madeline Stowe, Warren Fabro, Shaun Shimoda, Russell Omori, Mat Salinger

A four-hour miniseries set in Hawai'i in 1937, this drama deals with the improprieties of justice and the resultant civil unrest when four local youths are wrongly accused of the assault and rape of a Navy Lieutenant's wife. In the process of unraveling the facts of the case, a local captain of detectives falls in love with the young wife of a celebrated mainland attorney who is summoned to the Islands at the behest of the rape victim's powerful socialite mother. To complicate matters, the Navy Lieutenant commits the ultimate insurrection when he takes civilian police matters into his own hands.

Blood and Orchids was based very closely on the infamous real-life Massie case of 1931.

WAR AND REMEMBRANCE

ABC, 1988

D: Dan Curtis

T: Herman Wouk, Dan Curtis and Earl Wallace

P: Barbara Steele

Cast: Robert Mitchum, Polly Bergen, Jane Seymour, Sir John Gieguld, Hart Bochner

This 30-hour miniseries sequel to *The Winds Of War* miniseries begins with Pearl Harbor scenes and follows Victor "Pug" Henry (Mitchum), an American career Naval officer whose family becomes caught up in the horrors and triumphs of World War II. In the first chapters Pug and his son Byron (Bochner) are off fighting the war in the Pacific.

The Pacific war scenes were actually filmed during the summer of 1987 at Pearl Harbor, Hawai'i, and near the coast of O'ahu in Wai'anae Bay on a vintage Naval ship. The World War II-era vessels (the reserve tanker *Nodaway* and the Destroyer *Edwards*) were taken out of mothballs and refitted for the Pacific theatre re-creation. One hundred fifty

extras, many of them certified Hawai'i lifeguards, were hired for scenes involving sailors being rescued at sea after a Naval engagement. Most of the sub scenes were shot using the USS *Bowfin*, an actual historic submarine which was exhibited for tours next to the USS *Arizona* at Pearl Harbor. Although it hadn't been to sea for 18 years, the *Bowfin* was restored to seaworthiness after being fitted with an underwater bridle and was towed by an off-camera tugboat for scenes on the surface.

[1.] Four young Hawaiian sugar-plantation workers, played by Robert Andre, Warren Fabro, Russell Omori and Shaun Shimoda, are accused of rape in *Blood and Orchids*. Hawai'i's real-life Massie case was the island equivalent of the infamous Scottsboro Boys case, another racist miscarriage of justice.

[2.] Robert Mitchum as Victor "Pug" Henry is on the deck of a Navy ship in *War and Remembrance*, the sequel to *The Winds of War*. These ABC miniseries were among the most expensive productions in history.

Luis Reyes Collection

CHAPTER 6
Documentaries

PEARL HARBOR AND DECEMBER 8TH 1941 DOCUMENTARIES

This chapter examines nonfiction films and TV programs covering the attack on Pearl Harbor and the events leading up to it, as well as documentaries dealing with the Imperial offensive elsewhere in Asia and Oceania on December 8, 1941 (Tokyo time). According to USS *Arizona* National Park Ranger Daniel Martinez, up to nine new documentaries have been made to commemorate the 60th anniversary of that day of infamy. Most of the below have been released on video.

According to Robert C. Schmitt, author of the groundbreaking *Hawaii in the Movies, 1898-1959*, published by the Hawaiian Historical Society in 1988: "At least two semi-documentary films about Hawai'i were produced by the Japanese during World War II, *Hawai-Marei Oki Kaisen* (The War at Sea from Hawaii to Malaya) and *Shinju-Wan* (Pearl Harbor). Both were released in 1942. *Hawai-Marei Oki Kaisen* was a patriotic semi-documentary, directed by Kajiro Yamamoto, that re-created the years of preparation for the attack on Pearl Harbor, the training of pilots, the attack itself, and the Japanese sweep through Southeast Asia that followed it. Yamamoto, instructed by his government to make this picture, did so with such realism that—despite miniature sets and studio shots—Occupation authorities later mistook some of the scenes for the real thing. An American critic called the treatment of the December 7th attack "a brilliant miniaturization that allows us to witness the bombing at extremely close range." *Shinju-Wan* (Pearl Harbor), a Japanese film similarly re-creating the attack through miniatures, appears to be an excerpt from a longer picture, possibly *Hawai-Marei*

Oki Kaisen. A print of *Shinju-Wan* is in the collection of the Library of Congress.

WAR IN THE PACIFIC
U.S. Government, 1943-45

"This war documentary is an actual U.S. Navy photographic report," reads the video box for Volume Five of *War in the Pacific*—a multi-volume series about the island-hopping campaign and sea/air battles in the Pacific theatre. The 64-minute documentary is divided into four parts, the last of which has standard images and commentary regarding Yamamoto's Pearl Harbor foray. In addition to depicting the havoc wreaked, emphasis is placed on the repair work that salvaged planes and the *California*, *West Virginia*, *Tennessee*, *Nevada*, and other ships. The Alpha Video Distributors, Inc. video is in black and white and color, and preceding the Pearl footage are two accounts of the battle for Iwo Jima.

WHY WE FIGHT—WAR COMES TO AMERICA
U.S. War Department, 1944
P: Frank Capra

Leave it to good ol' Frank Capra, Hollywood's tribune of the common man, to produce a stirring series of seven documentaries explaining to Americans in and out of uniform "Why We Fight." Like *Blood on the Sun* screenwriter Lester Cole, Capra was (in general) one of Hollywood's exceptions to the rules when it came to propaganda. Capra directed the Depression Era populist classics *Mr. Deeds Goes To Town*, *Meet John Doe*, and above all, Jimmy Stewart in *Mr. Smith Goes To Washington* (written by Sidney Buchman, a Communist Party member later found guilty of contempt of Congress during the McCarthy Era). Instead of depending on racial demagoguery aimed at our baser instincts, Capra (usually) democratically appealed to our better angels. Most of the time, Capra persuasively argued that Americans should fight Japan not because our race is better than theirs, but rather because democracy is a superior form of government to fascism. Moreover, Capra stressed the quintessential Yankee love of liberty should form the basis of patriotism, not an American version of übermensch white supremacy. Capra may have been more sensitive to ethnic issues than most U.S. propagandists because he was an immigrant born in Sicily, which was ruled by Mussolini when Capra produced his wartime documentaries.

With the advent of WWII, Capra reenlisted in the Army (reaching the rank of Colonel), joining Hollywood's heroic John Ford, John Huston, George Stevens, William Wyler, Clark Gable, Henry Fonda, Myrna Loy, Robert Montgomery, Tyrone Power, and Jimmy Stewart, who "willingly put their careers on hold and themselves in harm's way," as Doherty notes in *Projections of War*. In the 834th Photo Signal Detachment Unit, Capra externalized the American fight against corrupt businessmen and politicians (like Edward Arnold and Claude Rains in *Mr. Smith*) during the Depression into what Capra called "the Great Struggle"—the crusade against fascism.

Prelude To War, the first in the *Why We Fight* series, won 1942's Best Documentary Oscar. Capra's later wartime agitprop included 1943's *Battle of Russia* and 1944's *The Negro Soldier*. The final *Why We Fight* installment, *War Comes to America*, presents a vision of America as a liberty-loving land of brotherhood. Members of many ethnic groups are depicted (except for indigenous Indians and Pacific Islanders) in the multiracial *Arsenal of Democracy*. The documentary chronicles America's isolationism, Neutrality Act, oil embargo, etc., as war approaches. Edward R. Murrow is seen and heard reporting on the Battle of Britain. In the conclusion, about five minutes of Pearl Harbor footage—intercut with Japanese envoys in Washington—shows those familiar images of Imperial bombardiers, Dorie Miller firing a machine gun, black smoke billowing over Battleship Row, and so on. FDR asks Congress for a declaration of war, and our most hallowed symbols—Old Glory, Lady Liberty, and the ringing Liberty Bell, with the "V" for victory sign superimposed on it—are seen, as "My country 'tis of thee/Sweet land of liberty," is sung.

War Comes to America's narrator asks if the U.S. rose up to fight fascism because of "our ancient antagonism to conquerors imposing their rule on others by force?" But even the *Why We Fight* series was not immune to the "yellow menace" ideology of the day. The narrator states, "We were in their way, we had to be removed, but in the Japanese way;" as an animated samurai knife is plunged into North America. This seventh *Why We Fight* volume (produced, but not directed by Capra) also uses the term "Jap," and claims that 260,000 Japanese in Brazil took their orders from Tokyo.

Nevertheless, most—if not all—of *Why We Fight*'s grand finale distinguishes itself with a systemic, as opposed to racial, critique of fascism and the reasons for opposing it. According to Doherty, Capra's sources for his *Why We Fight* series included Leni Riefenstahl's Nuremburg rally *Triumph of the Will* agitprop. Doherty's *Projections of War* states that the 1940s propaganda battle pitted Capra versus Riefenstahl, as Hollywood took on nazi propaganda minister Joseph Goebbels. Guess who ultimately triumphed?

THE WORLD AT WAR

The Office of War Information

P: The Office of War Information Bureau of Motion Pictures

The opening of *The World at War* (not to be confused with a similarly named BBC series of the 1970s) asserts "Nothing has been staged. Every scene in this record is authentic." As torrid classical music is heard, the U.S. Government-presented documentary makes what is a rather remarkable admission for a propaganda film: "The Editors are Americans, and therefore partisan…" The end title states that the celluloid material was derived from newsreels and "enemy films."

The documentary starts with Zeros on a carrier and the title "Pearl Harbor December 7, 1941." It then flashes back to Manchuria, as narrator Paul Stewart reminds American audiences that, while the U.S. didn't enter the war until late '41, other nations had already been fighting aggression for at least a decade by then. Encompassing Ethiopia, Spain, China, Czechoslovakia, Poland, and so on, the documentary details the Imperial, Italian, and nazi blitzkriegs. The film notes the power of cinema with a Goebbels-ordered pictorial record of "a barbarian symphony of devastation" wrought on a Dutch city, which the German Propaganda Minister had screened in neutral European and South American nations. Viewers can tell *The World at War* was made during WWII, because the Soviet leader Stalin, then an ally, is favorably depicted rallying the USSR. Shortly after V-Day, Stalin was vilified by U.S. propaganda, and some filmmakers who'd been asked by Washington to extol the virtues of the then-ally were persecuted by the postwar, Cold War U.S. government for having favorably depicted "Uncle Joe."

The World at War has an in-depth section on what is referred to as the "American island of Oahu." The familiar terrain of Japanese diplomats in Washington, bombs raining down on Battleship Row, pans and dolly shots revealing the carnage, and (but of course) Roosevelt's address before Congress, are shown. The Pearl sequence is followed by an interesting interventionist versus isolationist debate. A protester at an American bund rally disrupts a pro-nazi speaker and is pummeled. The Imperial invasion of the Philippines is also depicted, along with MacArthur's escape to Australia. There is a montage of industrial production as the Arsenal of Democracy backs the war effort. A montage of international troops shows the Pan-American nations joining the Allied cause, as the narrator declares that in "this war of the people…we were not alone…"

CRUSADE IN THE PACIFIC

ABC, 1951

S: Fred Feldkamp

P: Arthur B. Tourtellot

Shortly after WWII, two significant factors changed the American cultural and political landscape: the advent of TV as a mass medium, and the Cold War. The Good Fight made for good TV, and by 1949, the Second World War was must-see TV on Thursday nights. *Crusade in Europe* was a documentary series based on General Dwight Eisenhower's book of the same name. In that great entertainment industry tradition, *Crusade in the*

Pacific was the sequel. As the Korean War had begun by this time, this television crusade was placed in the context of postwar East-West rivalry. In addition to the U.S. National Archives and Office of Alien Property, sources included the U.S. Defense Department, the Australian Government Information Service, the British Information Service, the March of Time, and captured Japanese film. The series was copyrighted Time Inc. in 1951.

"The Pacific in Eruption" flashes back to Korea and Manchuria in 1931, and follows Imperial expansionism up to Pearl Harbor, which is shown with about a minute of bombers above Oʻahu, Admiral Nimitz, and what may be the most singular image of that carnage: the smoky carcass of the USS *Arizona*.

"Awakening in the Pacific" is fascinating because it details Washington's Manifest Destiny, the relentless "Westward Ho!" push past the Western coastline out into the Pacific. Shots of Alaska, Guam, and Hawaiʻi are glimpsed, including Diamond Head, the Royal Hawaiian Hotel, Waikīkī, the Captain Cook monument at Kealakekua Bay, downtown Honolulu, plantations, Pearl Harbor and other military fortifications, and (but of course) the inevitable lūʻau and hula dancers. War, this documentary tells us—not agriculture or tourism—is Hawaiʻi's principal industry. Japan includes shots of commentary on the state Shinto cult, emperor worship, sumo wrestling, the bushido warrior code, Tojo, and the expansionism which set Tokyo on a collision course with the Pacific Rim's other imperial powers.

"Rise of the Japanese Empire" kicks off with a banzai cheer and details Tokyo's expansionism from Micronesia to Manchuria to China, et al. Interestingly, footage reveals the reportedly accidental sinking of the U.S. gunboat *Panay* in the Yangtze by Japanese pilots. Narrator Westbrook Van Vorhees tells us, "Among the victims were the first American fighting men to lose their lives at the hands of the Japanese," in mid-December, 1937—four years before Pearl Harbor. Program 3 goes on to cover Tokyo's Tripartite Treaty with Hitler's Germany and Italy— Foreign Minister Matsuoka is shown on a balcony with Mussolini, who gives the stiff-armed fascist salute as the masses wildly cheer. There's discussion of U.S. economic restrictions imposed on Japan, and a detailed section on the last-minute December 1941 negotiations between Japanese diplomats and the State Department in Washington, D.C. Cut to: captured Japanese footage of the Imperial Task Force

300 miles from Hawai'i, pilots at Shinto shrines and then boarding their Zeros which take off from a carrier deck, and about a minute of Pearl Harbor carnage, as smoke engulfs the stricken *Arizona*. (The narrator claims 260 planes were destroyed, but in *Day of Infamy* Lord puts the number at 188.)

"America Goes To War" includes December 8, 1941 footage of Imperial forces landing on the Malayan Peninsula and attacking Hong Kong; the bombing of Singapore; and Thailand's surrender. "Rosie the Riveter," and other swing shifters and shipyard workers respond on the homefront, as the American people gear up for the struggle against fascism.

The *Crusade in the Pacific* TV series was sponsored by Regal Beer—proving once again that war is hell.

VICTORY AT SEA

An NBC Production in Cooperation with the U.S. Navy, 1952

D: M. Clay Adams

S: Henry Salomon, Richard Hauser

P: Henry Salomon

This two-hour or so documentary narrated by Leonard Graves concentrates on the Second World War from a maritime angle, and features an original musical score by Richard Rodgers (the composer of *South Pacific*, *The King and I*, *Oklahoma!*, etc.), performed by the NBC Orchestra. The action-packed *Victory At Sea* starts in 1939. A U-boat's periscope rises and the narrator declares: "for fascism to survive, it must kill." Crucial events in the European theatre through mid-1941 are depicted. "And now, the Pacific boils over," the narrator states, adding:

"Hawai'i—to Americans, an enchanted island territory… To the Japanese, Pearl Harbor, an enemy bastion. For two years, Europe has been at war. But in Honolulu, people talk of pineapples, sugarcane, money, and tourists… There is still time for one more aloha… to enjoy tropical skies and sweet music, flowered leis, the hula."

An unobstructed view of Diamond Head is glimpsed, as are palms, Mt. Olomana, downtown Honolulu, Aloha Tower, boat days on the *Lurline*, malihinis receiving leis, and hula dancers aboard a Naval vessel.

The film cuts to Japan, where "The ruling militarists hatch a fateful plan to eliminate the obstacle: sink the U.S. Navy." *Victory At Sea* has a great, exciting, long sequence on the preparations for, and execution of, the most comprehensive carrier-launched aerial attack up to that time. There's much intricate detail—the breaking of Japan's secret code; the Imperial envoys in Washington; the task force out at sea; and extensive footage of the raid itself: damaged ships with divers, welders, and shipyard workers (one of them was a teen-aged kid from Brooklyn named Eddie Sherman, who would become one of Hawai'i's most famous newspaper columnists…) undertaking "the most extraordinary salvage job in history… Dead ships sail again. A fleet has arisen from Pearl Harbor." A bugler plays taps as the *Arizona* is seen, and FDR rouses a downhearted nation with his declaration of war.

After the highly recommended, approximately 30-minute Pearl sequence there is a lull in the documentary, with footage about Navy training and convoys contending with Wolf Packs in the Atlantic. Once the film returns to the Pacific theatre, it picks up. First it shows Imperial conquest in the Philippines, Singapore, Hong Kong, Malaya, Shanghai, and more. Then the tide turns, with the Doolittle Raid, the Battle of the Coral Sea, Midway, etc. There's some breathtaking you-are-there war footage, including superb shots from a camera mounted on the underside of a plane of a wheel touching down, and cockpit point-of-view shots from a camera mounted behind a pilot taking off from a carrier. With cinematography like this, the Axis didn't stand a chance.

Victory at Sea was also shown as a series of half-hour television programs.

WORLD WAR II WITH WALTER CRONKITE

CBS, 1961

D: Eric Shapiro

S: Burton Benjamin, E.J. Kahn, Jr.

P: Burton Benjamin

Veteran CBS newsman Walter Cronkite observed the 20th anniversary of the Imperial offensive with a program about Takeo Yoshikawa, *The Man Who Spied on Pearl Harbor*. This shot-on-location CBS report is superb because Yoshikawa, the Imperial Naval Officer and secret agent, talks about his life story and espionage activities in Hawai'i while the news special graphically shows viewers the Pearl Harbor Naval Base and other O'ahu sites Yoshikawa describes. The scenes move from the USS *Arizona* (before the monument was built there) to Hickam (where bullet holes are glimpsed in a building) to a Pearl City pier and 'Aiea Heights, where Yoshikawa observed ship and plane deployments at Pearl.

The English-speaking intelligence officer (who speaks mostly in his native tongue in this report) assumed the name "Tadashi Marumara" and posed as a "sightseer" at all of the accessible Hawaiian Island sites. The agent states: "The place I wanted to see much was Pearl Harbor." His intelligence gathering included hiking, sightseeing flights from John Rogers Airport, fishing, swimming at beaches—where he scoped out anti-sub and torpedo nets—and working as a "Filipino" dishwasher at a Navy officers' mess hall. In these ways, largely via coded messages, Yoshikawa/Marumara supplied information to the Imperial Navy.

Twenty years later, the spy confesses he's not "ashamed" of his role in the sneak attack, but is, rather, "sad." Although he admits that Consul-General Kita of the Japanese consulate in Honolulu knew about his covert actions, Yoshikawa is adamant that he didn't have "any help" from the 150,000 people of Japanese ancestry in Hawai'i (more than half on O'ahu), who, he insists, "were faithful to America."

The Man Who Spied On Pearl Harbor became part of the CBS Video Library's *World War II With Walter Cronkite*, which also includes *Fortress Singapore*. This is another high-quality documentary narrated by Cronkite, who was a war correspondent in the European theatre. It begins with the CBS anchorman's sonorous voice gravely intoning: "The smoke still billowed at Pearl Harbor when the Japanese launched the second phase of their war. They began an attack aimed at the British Island of Singapore...Winston Churchill later called this battle the worst disaster in British history. When it was over, the British had lost... the Gibraltar of the Far East, the bastion of the empire, Singapore." According to the documentary, the Japanese attack on Singapore began half an hour after Pearl Harbor, on December 8, 1941 (Tokyo time).

This documentary has excellent footage shot on location in Singapore, Malaya (now Malaysia), and Thailand, showing coolies, British sahibs, General Yamashita (the Tiger of Malaya), and the Raffles Hotel, where Somerset Maugham once wrote about expat follies. It's a highly educational

chronicle, incorporating Japanese footage of the debacle that Churchill said caused him "a more direct shock" than any other WWII battle.

A few hours after the aerial assault on Pearl, Clark Field was likewise bombed. Cronkite narrates *Freedom for the Philippines*, a detailed account of the Imperial invasion of the then-U.S.-administered colony. An overview of the entire wartime Filipino experience is shown: Bataan, Corregidor, General MacArthur's vow "I shall return," guerrilla warfare, the Leyte Gulf offensive, MacArthur's return, Bataan death march survivors, street fighting in Manila, and ultimately, independence for the Philippines on July 4, 1946. The Pearl parley depicted in the Gregory Peck biopic "MacArthur"—wherein the General debated with FDR and the high command over Pacific theatre strategy—is also shown.

WWII With Walter Cronkite ends with the "Doolittle Raid" (as does 2001's big-screen *Pearl Harbor*). At Roosevelt's behest, on April 18, 1942, fifteen B-25s took off from the USS *Hornet*, 600 miles west of Japan, and dropped their payloads on Tokyo. This daring action sent Japan and America the message—loud and clear—that the Land of the Rising Sun wasn't invulnerable. Afterwards, Admiral Donald Duncan went to Pearl Harbor to tell his fellow Admirals, Chester Nimitz and Bull Halsey, about the daring Doolittle Raid. *World War II With Walter Cronkite* ends with a WWII montage that reprises three Pearl Harbor shots.

DECEMBER 7TH: DAY OF INFAMY

Narrated by Richard Basehart
David L. Wolper presentation
(Aired on ABC, 1963)

The events leading up to the December 7, 1941 Japanese attack on Pearl Harbor are documented in this historical one-hour special.

AMERICA GOES TO WAR

CBS

Cronkite wasn't the Tiffany Network's only veteran newsman to present WWII documentaries. Eric Sevareid narrates the Questar four-part video set *America Goes to War*. In the first installment, "While the Storm Clouds Gather," Sevareid indicts prewar America for its alleged naivete and isolationism (epitomized by "American First" member, famous pilot Charles Lindbergh). Sevareid virtually sneers at American pop culture as escapist entertainment: swing music, beauty pageants, Hollywood movies, and radio programs starring Bob Hope, Jack Benny, and George Burns and Gracie Allen. He condemns "America [for] indulg[ing] in mindless activities" and consumerism as the Nazis invade Europe. Familiar footage accompanies Sevareid's commentary about the events leading up the offensive against O'ahu. Interestingly, the CBS reporter states that the "Japanese envoys [in Washington]… had not been told that the Japanese Navy was sailing in secret and silence toward the Hawaiian Islands." Usually, it's implied that Admiral Nomura and Ambassador Kurusu were in on the surprise attack.

In any case, as scenes of the ravages wrought on O'ahu are shown, Sevareid declares: "The attack on Pearl Harbor ended the great American debate. Isolationism was no longer possible; its most vehement advocates could see that now. And America was finally united." Kate Smith sings "God Bless America" (really—no kidding; I couldn't make this stuff up if I tried!) Part two of the video set is called "Praise the Lord and Pass the Ammunition." It starts with Sevareid proclaiming: "…the attack on Pearl Harbor sent a bolt of energy through the people of the United States."

THE LIFE & DEATH OF A LADY

Bill Armstrong Productions, 1991

This is a biopic—not of a person but of a ship, the USS *Arizona*, produced to commemorate the 50th anniversary of the sinking of this famed vessel on Battleship Row.

REMEMBER PEARL HARBOR

CBS News, 1991

This two-hour television special with Charles Kuralt and General Norman Schwarzkopf was shown on the 50th anniversary of the attack on Pearl Harbor and included documentary footage, interviews with survivors and historians and previously unseen new footage. It also included readings utilizing the voice talents of such actors as Dustin Hoffman, Richard Dreyfuss and Kevin Costner. Also included was coverage of the official ceremonies commemorating the 50th anniversary at Pearl Harbor and an interview with then-U.S. President George Bush.

SHOOTING WAR

ABC, 2000

D: Richard Schickel

S: Richard Schickel

P: Steven Spielberg and Richard Schickel

Host/Narrator: Tom Hanks

This two-hour special told the story of the combat photographers of World War II through the use of the footage they shot and by way of interviews. The film opens with John Ford's depiction of Pearl Harbor and includes behind-the-scenes color footage of Ford with the miniatures on the Twentieth Century Fox studio backlot. (Aired, but of course, on December 7!)

WAIKIKI, IN THE WAKE OF DREAMS

FilmWorks/Pacific, 2000

D: Edgy Lee

S: Edgy Lee, Paul Berry

P: Edgy Lee, Michael Foley

Waikiki, In the Wake of Dreams is a social history of Waikīkī, from its Polynesian past as a royal reserve, healing place, and site for taro patches and fishponds; to a playground for beachboys, movie stars, and other rich and famous visitors; to its current status as one of the world's top tourist destinations. The 70-minute color and black-and-white documentary is a journey down memory lane and is chockfull of international and local celebs and notables, from Shirley Temple to Charlie Chaplin to surfer/Olympiad Duke Kahanamoku to Don Ho. Perhaps the most famous V.I.P. seen onscreen is President John F. Kennedy. In rare vintage footage, JFK visits the new USS *Arizona* Memorial, where he pays homage to the gallant fallen.

FDR is also shown visiting Hawai'i during the Roosevelt presidency. Using a car borrowed from Honolulu's biggest madam, General MacArthur meets with FDR and Admiral Nimitz to plan the island-hopping campaign. There is a WWII

[1]FDR in Papakōlea, 1934.

[2]FDR motorcade through downtown Honolulu, 1934.

1

Tai Sing Loo C1934 FDR Library / Photo courtesy of F[

President Roosevelt and sons at ʻIolani Palace, 1934.

Opposite page. President John Kennedy and Governor Burns (seated) rode
in an open-air limousine in a motorcade on Kalākaua Avenue
during an official visit to the Islands in June of 1963. Just five
months later, on November 22, 1963, the president was
assassinated while riding in a similar motorcade in Dallas, Texas.

sequence of wartime Waikīkī, when the Royal Hawaiian Hotel was used by the military. The aftermath of the Pearl Harbor devastation is glimpsed.

Waikiki's award-winning creator, Edgy Lee, is Hawai'i's leading nonfiction filmmaker.

HOW SHALL WE REMEMBER THEM?

National Park Service, 1992

D: Lance Bird

S: Bob Chenoweth, Curator, National Park Service; Daniel A. Martinez, National Park Service Historian, USS *Arizona* Memorial; Tom Kleiman, Harper Ferry Design Ferry Center N.P.S.

P: Lance Bird, The American Film Studies Center in N.Y.

This reflective 25-minute documentary using archival motion-picture footage and sound, original contemporary moving images, still photos, narration and animation is much more than a re-creation of the events of the day of infamy, and a moving tribute to the victims and survivors of the Pearl Harbor tragedy. *How Shall We Remember Them?* is viewed by visitors at the theatre on the land site of the USS *Arizona* Memorial prior to their ferry ride to the memorial above the sunken battleship itself, where hundreds of seamen are still entombed. An emotional piece, the documentary was considered for an Academy Award in 1994. In addition to providing historical background, *How Shall We Remember Them?* sets the proper tone for a visit to what is, after all, a solemn seaside cemetery. As the second most-traveled-to destination in the Aloha State, tourists in particular need to have imparted to them the appropriate history and attitude, so that visitors do not inappropriately act at the *Arizona* as they might behave at a tourist attraction like, say, Sea Life Park.

With a moving musical score by Robert Fitzsimmons, the short is an ideal companion piece for the Memorial—as one looks out across the still oil-slicked waters near where the USS *Missouri* is moored, and up into the skies, imagining the heavens filled with Zeros 60 years ago. The excursion offers a panoramic alpha and omega, as Pearl was the beginning of WWII for America, and the *Missouri*—where the treaty that ended the great crusade against fascism was signed in Tokyo Bay, September 2, 1945—marked the close of the global conflagration.

How Shall We Remember Them? chronicles what led up to the Imperial assault on O'ahu, noting—like most Pearl pics do—that "History was forever changed that morning" of December 7, 1941. Japan's 1930s invasions of Manchuria and China, as well as the Axis powers of the Tripartite Treaty are glimpsed (Hitler and Matsuoka appear on a balcony together), along with footage and sound derived from the National Archives, Movietone newsreels narrated by Lowell Thomas and others, plus other sources. The colonial collision between the European, American, and Japanese empires in the East is traced. "…the United States had interests in Asia too… We couldn't allow Japan to dominate the Pacific," says the narrator (Stockard Channing).

Washington's reaction to Tokyo's expansionism is shown: the U.S. Pacific Fleet is transferred from the West Coast to Pearl Harbor in order to deter Imperial aggression. Images of the 8,000-ton, armor-plated *Arizona*, with 14-inch guns that can fire a shell 20 miles, are also shown. Yet "the age of the battleship was at an end," the narrator warns. "The age of the aircraft carrier had arrived."

Enter "one man who knew it"—Admiral Isoruku Yamamoto, the Commander in Chief of the Japanese Combined Fleet who conceived the aerial assault on O'ahu. After the July 1941 Imperial invasion of French Indochina, FDR stops selling "Oil: the lifeblood of the Japanese war machine." General Hideki Tojo (described in the documentary's script as "Very grim and threatening") becomes Tokyo's Prime Minister in October 1941. In newsreel footage, Japanese envoy Kurusu and Nomura negotiate with Secretary of State Hull in Washington, as the Japanese task force departs November 26 across 4,000 miles of open sea for Hawai'i.

Shots of civilians and servicemen at play in the Islands are seen, as the "Pearly Shells" song is heard. The military's defensive posture on its Pacific outpost is depicted, along with shots of the soon-to-be disgraced Admiral Kimmel and General Short. Interestingly, the narrator notes: "The American military knew that a surprise Japanese attack on Hawai'i was possible, and they thought they were prepared." Close—but no cigar, as "the last night of peace slipped away," and the surprise aviation attack is shown in detail, raining devastation on an unprepared isle.

There are the archetypal shots of Imperial pilots, Zeros being readied, and dive-bombers, fighters, etc., taking off from carriers. Animation using a painting shows the *Ward* incident, wherein the warship depth-charged a midget sub. The outdoor 'Ōpana radar installation detects incoming planes, and Fort Shafter's Information Center tells the operators "Don't worry about it." The Battle of O'ahu is on, with archival footage—including shots from Japanese planes—revealing the onslaught against Kāne'ohe Bay Naval Air Station, Ford Island Naval Air Station, and Battleship Row. The USS *Oklahoma* capsizes, and in remarkable footage (by a Naval officer who'd just received a 16mm camera as a gift and was planning to lens morning colors), the *Arizona* is captured with a nine-second shot of it exploding, as "an armor-piercing bomb went through her deck and ignited the forward ammunition magazine."

Americans resist on land, sea, and in the air, sailors swim in burning oily water, the *Nevada* runs aground in order to avoid bottlenecking Pearl's narrow channel. The grim aftermath of Japan's juggernaut is revealed. In two hours "they had inflicted on the United States Navy the greatest disaster in its history." Twenty-one U.S. vessels were sunk or damaged, and 170 Army and Navy planes destroyed. On the U.S. side, 2,400-plus servicemen and civilians died, and 1,200 were wounded, while only 29 Imperial aircraft were downed and 55 airmen killed.

America's first prisoner of war is a midget-sub crewman, and his captured sub is shown. As in so many Pearl pictures, FDR delivers his stirring "date which shall live in infamy" speech. The song "Let's Remember Pearl Harbor" plays, as patriotic Yanks enlist in the military. The heroic salvage effort at Pearl is shown: but *Oklahoma*, *Utah*, and the *Arizona* cannot be rescued. As with so many films in this sub-genre, it closes with the inevitable American victories—Midway and Iwo Jima: we may have lost the battle, but not the war.

Contemporary shots of the USS *Arizona* Memorial, including the Flower Ceremony (with American and Japanese mourners) every December 7, are glimpsed. The narrator asks: "How shall we remember them, those who died? Mourn the dead. Remember the battle. Understand the tragedy. Honor the memory. Let our grief for the men of *Arizona* be for all those whose futures were taken from them on December 7th, 1941. Here they will never be forgotten."

Amen.

TO THE MEMORY OF THE GALLANT MEN HERE ENTOMBED AND THEIR SHIPMATES WHO GAVE THEIR LIVES IN ACTION ON DECEMBER 7, 1941 ON THE USS ARIZONA

Background. A stack of helmets reflect the loss of Americans killed in action in the Pacific war.

[1.] A wall of Vermont marble embraces the names of the USS *Arizona*. Montaged in the photo is wreckage from the ship.

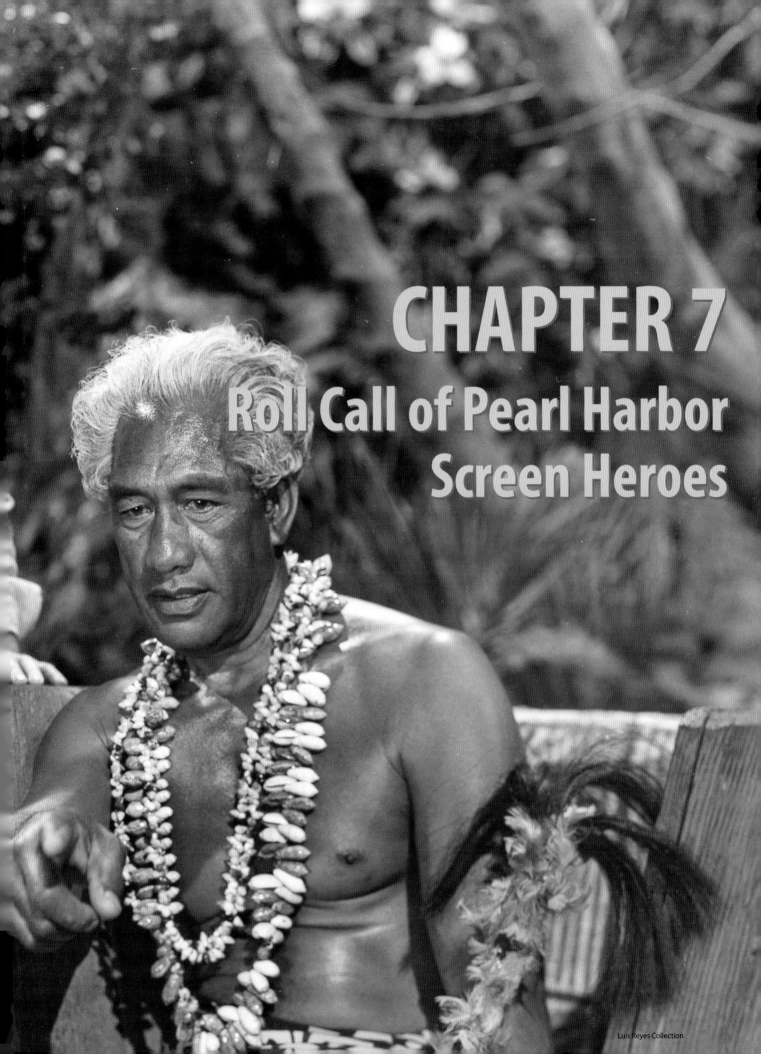

CHAPTER 7
Roll Call of Pearl Harbor Screen Heroes

ROLL CALL OF PEARL HARBOR SCREEN HEROES
BIOGRAPHIES

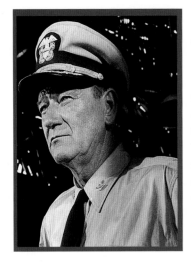

JOHN WAYNE
1907-1979

One of the icons of American cinema who came to personify the American hero and the American character, especially in Westerns and War dramas. Wayne probably spent as much time on-screen fighting the enemy during World War II as most GIs did on the battlefield.

His films included *The Flying Tigers* (1942), *The Fighting Seabees* (1944), *Reunion In France* (1943), *Back To Bataan* (1945), *They Were Expendable* (1945), and after the war *The Sands Of Iwo Jima* (1949), *Operation Pacific* (1951), *The Flying Leathernecks* (1951), *Jet Pilot* (1957), *Cast A Giant Shadow* (1966), *The Longest Day* (1962), *In Harm's Way* (1965), and *The Green Berets* (1968).

Ironically, Wayne did not serve in the military in real life. In WWII he was exempt from serving because he was the sole supporter of his four children. At the time the war broke out, Wayne's career was on the rise after he'd starred in John Ford's *Stagecoach* (1939) and he probably did not want to lose momentum after a decade of toiling in B-Westerns. As several U.S. Presidents told him, he did just as much for the image of America and for morale at home by the roles he undertook in the films that he made than if he had served at the front.

Previous page. The two Dukes— Kahanamoku and Wayne in *Wake of the Red Witch.*

GARY COOPER
1901-1961

Cooper played the quintessential American hero. He made his film debut in the classic aviation drama *Wings* (1927) and furthered his screen military service in *Sgt. York* (1941), *The Story Of Dr. Wassell* (1944), *Task Force* (1949), *U.S.S. Teakettle* (1951), and *The Court Martial Of Billy Mitchell* (1955).

ROBERT MONTGOMERY
1904-1981

A debonair leading man at MGM for many years, Montgomery's career included an outstanding military stint. Eight months before Pearl Harbor Montgomery enlisted in the U.S. Navy reserve at the rank of Lieutenant and served in London as a Naval attaché. After Pearl Harbor he was ordered to Newport for PT boat training. He served in both theaters of war and saw battle action in Guadalcanal and the Marshall Islands as well as on D-Day in Normandy. After 45 months of service he was made a full commander. His first film when back from the war was

They Were Expendable (1945). Montgomery pioneered unusual camera techniques in his feature directorial debut, *The Lady In The Lake* (1946), a film noir detective drama. He also directed the feature *The Gallant Hours* (1959), the story of Admiral Bull Halsey, starring James Cagney. He later served as advisor to President Eisenhower on matters relating to radio and television and created an acclaimed dramatic TV series during the 1950s.

ROBERT TAYLOR
1911-1969

A major star and handsome leading man for over 30 years at MGM, Taylor served as an Air Force flight instructor during World War II and narrated the Academy Award-winning documentary *The Fighting Lady* (1944). He starred as Sgt. Dane in *Bataan* (1943), and was seen in uniform in such films as *Waterloo Bridge* (1940), *Flight Command* (1940), *Stand By For Action* (1942), and *D-Day, The Sixth Of June* (1956).

BURT LANCASTER
1913-1994

The handsome athletic actor's career spanned four decades and a wide range of roles. Lancaster served in the U.S. Army during World War II. He was seen to best advantage in uniform in James Jones' *From Here To Eternity* (1953). He also donned a marine uniform for *South Sea Woman* (1953), and an Army uniform for *Seven Days In May* (1964), *Go Tell The Spartans* (1978), and in *Twilight's Last Gleaming* (1977).

GLENN FORD
1916-

The Canadian-born actor enlisted in the U.S. Marine Corps in 1942. He became a full commander in the U.S. Naval Reserve and served two tours of active duty with the Marine III Amphibious Force in Vietnam. His most famous film credits include *Gilda* (1946), *The Big Heat* (1953), *Blackboard Jungle* (1955), and *3:10 To Yuma* (1957). He saw military screen service in *Teahouse Of The August Moon* (1956), *Don't Go Near The Water* (1957), *Torpedo Run* (1958), *Imitation General* (1958), *Is Paris Burning* (1966), and *Midway* (1976).

GREGORY PECK
1916-

Peck personified General Douglas MacArthur in the film *MacArthur* (1977), and was an Army Air Corps flyer in the classic *Twelve O'Clock High* (1949). His other military credits include *Pork Chop Hill* (1959), *On The Beach* (1959) *Guns Of Navarone* (1961), and *Captain Newman M.D.* (1963)

FRANK SINATRA
1915-1998

Before his Academy Award-winning performance in the Best Supporting Actor category as Private Maggio in *From Here To Eternity* (1953), Sinatra donned a sailor suit for two classic MGM musicals, *Anchors Aweigh* (1945) and *On The Town* (1949). He later continued his screen military service as a GI in *Kings Go Forth* (1958), *Never So Few* (1959), *The Manchurian Candidate* (1962), *Von Ryan's Express* (1965), and *None But The Brave* (1965), which he also directed.

CHARLTON HESTON
1926-

Although he served in the Army during the Big One, Heston has been in a World War II uniform in only two films: *Midway* (1976), as a Naval officer and *The Pigeon That Took Rome* (1962) as a GI. He has played an American soldier of other periods, such as the Civil War Union cavalry officer in *Major Dundee* (1965) and as a Marine stationed in China in *55 Days At Peking* (1963). He played a nuclear submarine captain in *Gray Lady Down* (1977).

KIRK DOUGLAS
1916-

Douglas enlisted in the Navy and served during World War II. On-screen he served as a naval officer in *In Harm's Way* (1965), and in *The Final Countdown* (1980). His other on-screen military service has included an Army Colonel in *Seven Days In May* (1964), as General Patton in *Is Paris Burning* (1966), and as a general in *Top Secret Affair* (1957). Douglas portrayed the real-life Col. Mickey Marcus, one of the founding defenders of the state of Israel, in *Cast A Giant Shadow* (1966). His other credits include *Town Without Pity* (1961) and *The Hook* (1962). He starred in the Stanley Kubrick antiwar movie *Paths Of Glory* (1957).

JANE RUSSELL
1921-

Dark, busty, earthy and all woman, Russell was discovered by Howard Hughes. She played prostitute Mamie Stover in the Honolulu-set film *The Revolt Of Mamie Stover* (1956). Among her many classic film credits are *Gentleman Prefer Blondes* (1953), *The Outlaw* (1941), and *The Tall Men* (1955).

DONNA REED
1921-1986

She played a nurse in *They were Expendable* (1945) and the prostitute Lorene in *From Here To Eternity* and won a Best Supporting Actress Oscar in 1954 for the role. She is perhaps best known to baby boomers as Jeff's mom in the television series *The Donna Reed Show* (ABC, 1958-1966) and to contemporary audiences for her role as Jimmy Stewart's devoted wife in the Frank Capra classic *It's A Wonderful Life* (1946).

JEFF CHANDLER
1918-1961

Chandler's World War II screen credits include *Red Ball Express* (1952), the story of the U.S. Army Transportation Corps during World War II that was comprised of largely African-American drivers, *Away All Boats* (1956), as the captain of a naval attack transport, and as General Frank Merrill in Samuel Fuller's *Merrill's Marauders* (1962), his last film.

JEFFREY HUNTER
1927-1969

The handsome young actor starred in *Sailor Of The King* (1953), *In Love and War* (1958), *Hell To Eternity* (1960), and *No Man Is An Island* (1962). He is best remembered for his role in *The Searchers* (1956), and as Jesus in *King Of Kings*.

RANDOLPH SCOTT
1903-1987

Scott appeared as a Marine in *To The Shores Of Tripoli* (1942) and in *Gung Ho!* (1943) as a Marine colonel. He was best known for his work in Westerns, though he played a variety of roles from romantic lead to co-star in such films as *Ride The High Country* (1962), *The Tall T* (1957), *The Spoilers* (1942), *Rebecca Of Sunnybrook Farm* (1938), *Western Union* (1941), and *Jesse James* (1939).

PATRICIA NEAL
1926-

Patricia Neal played a Naval nurse opposite John Wayne in *Operation Pacific* (1951) and played a similar role as a nurse opposite John Wayne 15 years later in *In Harm's Way* (1965). It was almost like a continuation of their relationships and roles in the earlier film. Neal won an Oscar in 1963 as Best Actress for her role opposite

Paul Newman in *Hud*.

HENRY FONDA
1905-1982

Fonda served in the U.S. Navy during World War II and lent his vocal talents as one of the narrators of the documentary *The Battle Of Midway*. He will forever be identified for the role he created on the Broadway stage as *Mr. Roberts* and later in the 1955 film version of the celebrated play. Fonda played Admiral Nimitz twice, first in *In Harm's Way* (1964), and later in *Midway* (1976). The actor also donned a GI uniform for *The Battle Of The Bulge* (1965) and *The Longest Day* (1962). He was also a Naval officer in the comedy *Yours, Mine and Ours*, in which he starred opposite Lucille Ball.

TYRONE POWER
1914-1958

During World War II, Power was a Marine Transport pilot in the South Pacific. The handsome actor who was under long-term contract at Twentieth Century Fox studios starred in *A Yank In The RAF* (1941), *Crash Dive* (1943), and *An American Guerrilla In The Philippines* (1951).

ELVIS PRESLEY
1935-1977

While Elvis starred in many Hawai'i-set films, including *Blue Hawaii*, *Girls! Girls! Girls!*, and *Paradise, Hawaiian Style*, his connection to Pearl Harbor was much more personal. When a Los Angeles newspaper ran an article outlining how $200,000 was needed to complete a memorial in Pearl Harbor at the site of the sunken USS *Arizona*, the King responded. In 1961, the former G.I. turned rebellious rock-and-roller gave a charity concert at the Pearl Harbor Bloch Arena, raising more than $57,000 to help construct the USS *Arizona* Memorial.

BIBLIOGRAPHY

Allen, Helena G. *Kalakaua: Renaissance King*. Honolulu: Mutual Publishing, 1995

Astor, Gerald. *Crisis In The Pacific*. New York: Donald I. Fine Books, 1996

Barry, Iris. *D.W. Griffith*. Museum Of Modern Art, New York: Doubleday and Co., 1940, 1965

Basinger, Jeanine. *The World War II Combat Film: Anatomy Of a Genre*. New York: Columbia University Press, 1986

Beigel, Harvey. *The Fleet's In: Hollywood Presents The U.S. Navy In World War II*. Missoula, Montana: Pictorial Histories Publishing Co., 1994

Belafonte, Dennis and Alvin H. Marill. *The Films Of Tyrone Power*. N.J.: Citadel Press, 1979

Bergan, Ronald. *The United Artist Story*. New York:Crown Publisher, 1986

Bergman, Andrew. *We're In The Money: Depression America and Its Films*. New York: Harper/Colophon Books, 1972

Biskind, Peter. *Easy Rider, Raging Bulls: How the Sex-Drugs-and Rock and Roll Generation Saved Hollywood*. New York: Simon and Schuster, 1998

Bogle, Donald. *Toms, Coons, Mulattoes, Mammies, & Bucks, An Interpretive History of Blacks in American Films*. New York: Continuum, 1990

Brook, Tim and Earle Marsh. *The Complete Directory to Prime Time Network and Cable TV Shows 1946–Present*. New York: Ballantine Books, 1995

Carnes, Mark C. *Past Imperfect: History According To The Movies*. New York: Henry Holt and Co., 1995

Churchhill, Winston S. *The Grand Allaince*. Boston: Houghton Mifflin Co., 1950

Conroy, Hilary and Wray, Henry. *Pearl Harbor Reexamined: Prologue to The Pacific War*. Honolulu: University of Hawai'i Press, 1990

Costello, John. *The Pacific War 1941-1945*. New York: Quill, 1981

Davenport, Kiana. *Song Of The Exile*. New York: Ballantine Books, 1999

Daws, Gavan. *Shoal Of Time: A History of the Hawaiian Islands*. Honolulu: University of Hawai'i Press, 1968

Doherty, Thomas. *Projections Of War: Hollywood, American Culture and WWII*. New York: Columbia University Press, 1993

Dudley, Michael Kioni and Keoni Keoloha Agard. *A Call For Hawaiian Sovereignty*. Honolulu: Na Kane Oka Malo Press, 1993

Eames, John Douglas. *The MGM Story*. New York: Crown Publishers, 1979

Eyles, Allen. *John Wayne and The Movies*. NJ: AS Barnes and Co., 1976

Gorden, Bernard. *Hollywood Exile, or How I Learned to Love The Blacklist*. Austin: University of Texas Press, 1999

Guttmacher, Peter. *Elvis: The King and His Movies*. New York: Friedman/Fairfax Publishing, 1997

Katz, Ephraim. *The Film Encyclopedia*. New York: Harper Perennial, 1994

LaForte Robert S. and Ronald E. Murcello. *Remembering Pearl Harbor*. Wilmington, Delaware: Scholarly Resources Inc,1991

Lili'uokalani. *Hawaii's Story*. Honolulu: Mutual Publishing,1990

Lord, Walter. *Day Of Infamy*. New York: Holt, Rineheart & Winston, 1957

Marill, Alvin H. *The Films Of Anthony Quinn*. NJ: Citadel Press, Secaucus, 1975

McCann, Graham. *Rebel Males, Clift, Brando and Dean*. NJ: Rutgers University Press, 1993

McCarty, John. *The Complete Films of John Huston*. NJ: Citadel Press, 1987

Mita, Robert T. M.D. and Douglas Peebles. *ABC Hawaii: An Illustrated Reference Guide*. Honolulu: Mutual Publishing, 1994

Oliver, Anthony Michael. *Hawaii: Fact and Reference Book*. Honolulu: Mutual Publishing, 1995

Prange Gordon W. *At Dawn We Slept: The Untold Story of Pearl Harbor*. New York: McGraw-Hill Books Co., 1981

Reyes, Luis I. and Ed Rampell. *Made In Paradise: Hollywood's Films Of Hawaii and The South Seas*. Honolulu: Mutual Publishing, 1995

Rhodes, Karen Booking. *Hawaii Five-0: An Episode Guide and Critical History*. Jefferson, North Carolina: McFarland & Company, 1997

Rusbridger, James and Eric Nave. *Betrayal at Pearl Harbor: How Churchill Lured Roosevelt into WWII*. New York: Summit Books, 1991

Schmitt, Robert C. *Hawaii In The Movies 1898-1959*. Honolulu: Hawaiian Historical Society, 1988

Slackman, Michael. *Target: Pearl Harbor*. Honolulu: University Of Hawai'i Press, 1990

Truffaut, Francois. *Hitchcock*. New York: Simon & Schuster, 1967

Wills, Gary. *John Wayne's America: The Politics Of Celebrity*. New York: Simon & Schuster, 1997

Wood, Houston. *Displacing Natives*. Lanham, Maryland: Rowman & Littlefield Publishers Inc, 1999

Zinnemann, Fred. *An Autobiography: A Life In the Movies*. New York: Charles Scribner & Sons, 1992

PEARL HARBOR VIDEOTAPE AND DVD FILM SOURCE

Videotape and DVD are two most popular formats for viewing old films at home today. Pearl Harbor film titles available on videotape and/or DVD are listed here along their distributors. N/A means that the film is not available.

Movie Title	Videotape Source	DVD Source
A		
Across the Pacific	MGM/UA Home video	N/A
Admiral Yamamoto	N/A	N/A
Air Force	Key Home Video	N/A
An American Guerilla	N/A	N/A
Away All Boats	Universal/MCA Home Video	N/A
B		
Back To Bataan	Turner Home Entertainment	N/A
Bataan	MGM/Warner Bros. Home Video	MGM/Warner Bros. DVD
Battle at Bloody Beach	N/A	N/A
Big Jim McLain	Warner Bros. Home Video	N/A
Blood on the Sun	Hollywood Home Theatre	Laser Light DVD
C		
The Caine Mutiny	Columbia/TriStar Home Entertainment	Columbia/TriStar DVD
The Court Martial	Republic Home Video	N/A
Crimson Tide	Touchstone Home Video	Touchstone DVD
Cry of Battle	N/A	N/A
D		
December 7th	Kit Parker Home Video	Kit Parker DVD
Dive Bomber	MGM/Warner Bros.	N/A
E		
Empire of the Sun	Warner Home Video	Warner DVD
F		
The Fighting Seabees	Republic Home Video	Republic DVD
The Fighting Sullivans	Ivy Home Video	Roan DVD
The Final Countdown	Vestron Home Video	N/A
The Flying Tigers	NTA Home Video	Artisan DVD
From Here to Eternity	Columbia/Tristar Home Entertainment	Columbia/Tristar DVD
G		
Gung Ho	Mandacy Home Video	N/A

Movie Title	Videotape Source	DVD Source
H		
Hell to Eternity	Key Video/CBS Fox	N/A
Hell's Half Acre	N/A	N/A
Here Comes The Navy	N/A	N/A
I		
I Bombed Pearl Harbor	Ivy Home Video	N/A
Imperial Navy	Ivy Home Video	N/A
In Harm's Way	Paramount Home Video	Paramount DVD
In the Navy	MCA/Universal Home Video	N/A
M		
MacArthur	MCA/Universal Home Video	N/A
Manila Calling	N/A	N/A
Midway	MCA/Universal Home Video	MCA/Universal DVD
N		
1941	MCA/Universal Home Video	MCA/Universal DVD
Navy Blues	N/A	N/A
No Man Is an Island	N/A	N/A
O		
Operation Pacific	Warner Bros. Home Video	N/A
P		
Pearl Harbor	Buena Vista Home Video	Buena Vista DVD
R		
Radio Days	Orion Home Video	N/A
Remember Pearl Harbor	N/A	N/A
The Revolt of Mamie Stover	Other World Video	N/A
Run Silent, Run Deep	MGM/United Artists Home Video	N/A
S		
Sailor Beware	N/A	N/A
Sands of Iwo Jima	Republic Home Video	Republic DVD
Secret Agent of Japan	N/A	N/A
So Proudly We Hail	MCA/Universal Home Video	N/A
Submarine Raider	N/A	N/A
Swing Shift	Warner Home Video	Warner DVD
T		
Task Force	Warner Bros. Home Video	N/A
They Were Expendable	MGM/Warner Home Video	MGM/Warner DVD
Tora! Tora! Tora!	Fox Home Video	Fox DVD
Torpedo Run	MGM Home Video	N/A
To The Shores Of Tripoli	Fox Video	N/A
U		
Under Siege	Warner Bros. Home Video	Warner Bros. DVD
Up Periscope	Warner Bros. Home Video	Warner Bros. DVD
W		
Wackiest Ship in the Navy	Columbia/Tristar Home Entertainment	N/A
Wake Island	MCA/Universal Home Video	N/A
The Wings of Eagles	MGM/Warner Home Video	MGM/Warner DVD
Wings Over Honolulu	N/A	N/A

MBER
ARBOR

C PICTURE

WITH

DONALD M. BARRY
ALAN CURTIS
FAY McKENZIE

SIG RUMAN · IAN KEITH

RHYS WILLIAMS · DIANA DEL RIO

ABOUT THE AUTHORS

ED RAMPELL

When Ed Rampell's ancestors were drafted to fight during the Russo-Japanese war, they fled Kiev in 1904 and came to America. Rampell's cousin Mario and uncles Miguel and Larry were Filipino guerrillas during WWII. Rampell's Uncle Martin loaded the A-bomb onto the Enola Gay at Tinian. His uncle Arnie was a radio operator at Unishima, Japan during the Korean War.

Rampell majored in cinema at Hunter College, Manhattan, in 1976, and went on to live in Tahiti, Samoa, Guam, Micronesia, and Hawai'i. Rampell reported for ABC News' *20/20*, Radio Australia, *Pacific Islands Monthly*, *Honolulu Weekly*, *Pacific Business News*, *Islands*, etc., co-authored *Tu Galala, Social Change in the Pacific* and *Made In Paradise, Hollywood's Films of Hawaii and the South Seas*, and was the only full-time writer featured in the University of Hawai'i Press' *Autobiography of Protest in Hawaii*. Rampell emerged as one of the Pacific Islands' foremost full-time writers, and moved to Los Angeles in 1999 to further his writing career. Since his arrival in L.A., Rampell has gone on to write for *Variety*, the Writers Guild of America's *Written By* magazine, and has a screenplay about the Pacific in development.

LUIS I. REYES

Luis I. Reyes is a veteran film and television publicist whose credits include *The Lonely Guy, Zoot Suit, Stand and Deliver, American Me, Hoosiers, The Josephine Baker Story*, TNT's *The Cisco Kid* and New Line Cinema's *My Family* as well as the CBS-TV series *Dr. Quinn: Medicine Woman* and Showtime's *Resurrection Blvd.*

An author, film historian and archivist, Reyes is co- author, along with Ed Rampell, of *Made In Paradise: Hollywood's Films Of Hawaii and The South Seas* (Honolulu: Mutual Publishing 1995). Reyes also is the co-author, with Peter Rubie, of *Hispanics In Hollywood: An Encyclopedia Of Film and Television* (New York: Garland Publishing 1994, Los Angeles: Lone Eagle, 2000)

An acknowledged authority on the history of Hispanics in Hollywood and on Hawai'i in the movies, Reyes is often used as a reference source by the major media. The author has been featured on CNN's *Showbiz Today*, A & E Network's *Biography* series, "E" Entertainment television and Fox's *Collectibles Show* as well as in *USA Today, The Los Angeles Times, The San Francisco Chronicle, The Honolulu Advertiser* and *The New York Daily News*. He has also lectured on film at UCLA and California State University, Northridge, and is a member of the Directors Guild of America and The Publicists Guild. His articles on film have appeared in *The Los Angeles Times, The Oakland Tribune*, United Airlines' *Hemispheres* magazine and *Hawaii* magazine.

Reyes is a graduate of University of The Pacific, Stockton, California where he earned a BA degree in Education and Inter-American studies from Elbert Covell College.

He makes his residence in the small agricultural town of Fillmore in Ventura County, sixty miles Northwest of Los Angeles, with his wife Ronda, son Little Lui and daughter Arlinda Marie.